Comediology

Chris S. Tabish
with
Kurtis Matthews

Copyright © 2018 Chris S. Tabish with Kurtis Matthews.

All rights reserved. No part of this book may be used or reproduced by any means, graphic, electronic, or mechanical, including photocopying, recording, taping or by any information storage retrieval system without the written permission of the author except in the case of brief quotations embodied in critical articles and reviews.

Balboa Press books may be ordered through booksellers or by contacting:

Balboa Press
A Division of Hay House
1663 Liberty Drive
Bloomington, IN 47403
www.balboapress.com
1 (877) 407-4847

Because of the dynamic nature of the Internet, any web addresses or links contained in this book may have changed since publication and may no longer be valid. The views expressed in this work are solely those of the author and do not necessarily reflect the views of the publisher, and the publisher hereby disclaims any responsibility for them.

The author of this book does not dispense medical advice or prescribe the use of any technique as a form of treatment for physical, emotional, or medical problems without the advice of a physician, either directly or indirectly. The intent of the author is only to offer information of a general nature to help you in your quest for emotional and spiritual well-being. In the event you use any of the information in this book for yourself, which is your constitutional right, the author and the publisher assume no responsibility for your actions.

Any people depicted in stock imagery provided by Getty Images are models, and such images are being used for illustrative purposes only.
Certain stock imagery © Getty Images.

This book is a work of non-fiction. Unless otherwise noted, the author and the publisher make no explicit guarantees as to the accuracy of the information contained in this book and in some cases, names of people and places have been altered to protect their privacy.

Print information available on the last page.

ISBN: 978-1-9822-0892-9 (sc)
ISBN: 978-1-9822-0890-5 (hc)
ISBN: 978-1-9822-0891-2 (e)

Library of Congress Control Number: 2018908500

Balboa Press rev. date: 01/17/2019

Contents

Foreword vii

Introduction ix

Why Are You Here? 1

Why Comedy? 17

You've Got to Feel It to Make Them Believe It 45

Presence 61

Competition versus Creation 79

Vulnerability 97

Feedback. It's Not about You. No, Really Though. 109

Less Is More 121

Finding Your Voice 129

Epilogue 143

Acknowledgments 145

Sources..147

About the Authors.. 151

Foreword

I'm Kurtis Matthews. I'm a professional comedian, executive comedy coach and stand up teacher to approximately 10,000 ungrateful comedy students. Let me congratulate you on investing into yourself and this book. Not only will you get a treasure trove of useful and fun information you also get to read this fantastic foreword. And for that my friends, you are welcome!

Chris Tabish came to the San Francisco Comedy College many years ago. I didn't think much of him at the time as he was just one of the many who come to me interested in becoming a stand-up comedian, are forced to attend by therapist or are going through some weird midlife crisis they would like to solve without destroying their family. To be honest, most people with adequate love in their life, stimulating jobs and normal self-worth don't think to themselves "Hey wouldn't it be fun to get onstage in front of semi-inebriated strangers in low end bars and share my opinions!? Luckily the corporate world had beat the self-worth out of Chris, he was ready to learn, and we quickly became friends!

After some time, Chris and I began to wonder if some workplaces might just be low end bars one is forced to perform in 50 weeks a year and why isn't there more joy in every worker and workplace? We wrestled with these questions for many years and while I continued teaching many to be funnier, Chris embarked upon his own internal comedic journey and quest for contentment. I believe he became obsessed with wondering how many of the lessons of stand-up comedy and attributes of funny people could be applied to most corporate interactions. Sadly, this is when he stopped talking to people, retreated to a cave and began carving algebraic equations into stalactites (those are the ones on top). The following is a result of his vision quest!

I was honored to work with Chris. This is a great book filled with solid comedy theory, inspiration and astute observation of the human conditions presented by a great corporate citizen and a very funny man! Enjoy!

- Kurtis Matthews
San Francisco, California

Introduction

Do you love what you do for a living? Do you jump out of bed totally excited like it's Christmas and you're a kid who has been good all year? And your bed is coincidentally on fire? In one-on-one meetings, does your boss randomly applaud your performance while offering coconut bonbons covered in dark chocolate and stock option grants? When you arrive home at night, do your family and neighbors stand in front of the house with picket signs reading, "We are so grateful for your cost-effectiveness" while blasting Queen's "We Are The Champions"?

No? Hmmm . . . strange.

Well then, let me ask you: have you ever been unfulfilled in your professional life? No? Really?! Are you a professional Valium tester? I knew it! Perhaps you need a partner. Call me.

Oh wait, I just realized. You're on Valium. You could care less about me. Never mind.

For the rest of you "normal people" out there, if you're anything like me, you've realized the following:

A) You must make a living. That is, unless you actually *do* receive that check from Nigeria or Bill Gates for all of those emails you forwarded to your friends back in 1997.

B) You're going to be working for a very long time. No, I mean a REALLY LONG TIME. To better understand this, calculate the time it takes for the person in front of you to finish peeing, or whatever the hell he's doing in there that's taking FOR EVAH! Multiply that by a gazillion. Times it by pi. Pause. Times it by pi again for safe measure, 'cause, you know, I heard that one time in algebra class. Then add in any of the *Transformer* movies. Yeah, that's about how long you'll be working.

C) You might like what you do, maybe even love it, but at times it will be a stank-fest and you'll want to throw in the towel and hide like a Minnesota Vikings field goal kicker. Or, for you non-football fans out there, like you are *the* person with a book at a monster truck rally..

D) You must face reality. There are two things I love—*The 4-Hour Workweek* and dragons. But alas, I'm not a child anymore and can't be fooled by fictitious shenanigans. At some point in our lives, we must recognize once and for all there's no such thing as the four-hour work week! Dragons, however, do exist on *Game of Thrones*. In fact there are three—I've seen 'em.

E) You're not George Clooney or Angelina Jolie. That said, if you *are* George or Angelina and you're actually reading this, call me—I'll be testing Valium.

Realizing all of the above in 2010 was difficult. I was working at a Fortune 500 company in a very stressful corporate role—is there any other kind? I was always tense. My day was packed with meetings that frankly felt more like sentencings. They went something like this. "For your lack of being able to anticipate our ad hoc and rat-hole inquiries, you will receive fourteen action items. You will need to complete these as soon as possible but not before we change our minds on what we want. Furthermore, you must continue to dress like a 1950s tax accountant."

I also remember feeling like I couldn't reply naturally and needed to respond like a "responsible corporate citizen," whatever that means. And don't try this at home—seriously, it's weird. Whenever you observe yourself reacting to an insult, threat, or other corporate dysfunction like George McFly from *Back To The Future*, well, congratulations—you're conforming to Corporate America! "Oh yes Biff, thanks for the intimidation *and* harassment; that's some impressive multi-tasking. Oh yeah, I'll have those papers for you first thing in the morning if you'd be so kind as to unshackle me from the school radiator."

I never felt I had the freedom to engage the way I saw fit. I didn't even feel empowered to tell people what I really thought about their ideas. It felt so restrictive and unauthentic—like living in a personality condom. Thoughts like, "What are you thinking, jackass?!" came out of my mouth sounding like, "Well, John, if you *do* pop out of an oversized cake at the company meeting while yelling, "Your Christmas bonuses have arrived, y'all!", you might just want to be holding checks in your hand, be completely out of the cake, and wearing pants, that's all."

By the way, I'm not claiming to be a victim here. No one forced me to interact this way. This was my choice and I clearly did it. I don't know why I felt the pressure in the first place and why I gave in to it. Nor could I tell you why I breathe air, other than it's there and quite convenient, given my nose set above my mouth and what have you. Publicly, it was all very professional and secure. I had the life. I even portrayed that naïve look of hopeful optimism while posing for corporate pictures. Inside, however, I was miserable.

Living in corporate America, it seemed, was to exist among a different breed of people. Perhaps I was an amiable golden retriever surrounded by aggressive pit bulls. Sure, I could fetch a ball just as fast and with less orb-slobber than they could. But, unlike them, I might be distracted by a nice patting or a good butt sniffing. They were all business—relentlessly latching onto a target regardless of the consequences. That said, I couldn't confirm that I was different, because maybe they were just "playing their part," too. Were they just *acting* like pit bulls? In a situation like this one, it's hard to tell what's real. It really is like being a dog. You have no means to acquire a mirror, no opposable thumbs to hold it, and all the good information is secretly stashed up someone else's butt.

I was different. Or at least, I *felt* very different, whether I was or not. I often thought, professional life *has* to be more fulfilling, more fun, more humanistic than this. After all, weren't those guys in the coal mines always whistling?

I remember walking into the office every Monday morning. My nerves would kick in while my digestive tract apparently initiated the hosting of the NASCAR Sprint Cup. I always had this overwhelming sense of anxiety, wondering what was going to blow up in my face that day. I felt shameful just showing up for work, as though I had done something wrong and was going to be found out. Any minute the boss was going to come up and say, "Okay, they're all in the plane ready to jump—you loaded the parachutes, right?" What?! Someone was depending on *me* to load parachutes? I can't even fold a blanket!

The crazy thing was, I was really good at what I did. I had always been evaluated very high. (Not to say I actually *was* high, mind you, just evaluated as such. We'll call it "evaluation high" . . . it was "totally legal," ya know. . . .) I had steadily risen through the ranks and had even won prestigious awards, for which I'd only had to make out with three of my bosses (that was a joke, Mom; it was straight to intercourse). But it was irrelevant. My anxiety was not fact based but, instead, was part of the mental transition I went through to enter the world of pit bulls. This was the price I was paying for not being real, not being myself.

Was this the way my life was supposed to be? Was I resigned to living a life swimming against the current? Was it just me? Perhaps all the other pit bulls started out as golden retrievers and decided to smarten up before their next ball was stolen? I was confused. On one hand, I was a well-compensated professional with plenty of opportunity in sight. On the other, I felt about as lost as Dorothy in Oz being surrounded by the Lollipop Guild. So, let me get this straight. These little dudes just come out of nowhere and sing in perfect harmony? Oh, I see. Yeah, that makes complete sense.

At the time, I heard a quote that really resonated with me: "Life is a shit sandwich and every day you take another bite." Ahhhh . . . how's that for some motivation?! And no small wonder people die of cholera. It also might explain why Nutella was invented.

While *I* was resigned to pay the heavy toll for the sweet, sweet luxury of Home Depot upgrades and funnel cakes, I hadn't realized the effects my corporate shame had on my family. They could see it in my face, my eyes, and my ever-enlarging midsection girth (yeah, sorry about using *that* word). I could make the sacrifice for money to take care of my family's well-being. But, ultimately, *why was I doing this?* What was the end goal and what was I teaching my children? I'm spending money to "take care" of them and save money for their college so they could . . . what? Be just like me? Oh my God, really? No! I wanted them to *live* their dreams, not be confined to a pit bull cage, suppressing their inner golden retrievers.

I realized that it was time to make a decision. I needed to live my dreams, both for me and to set an example for my children. I decided right there and then that I was not going to live in the world of aggressive pit bulls—or if I was, it was going to be on my terms, as a golden retriever, not an emulated pit bull. I would no longer eat the shit sandwich. I no longer wanted to live the life of a *Dilbert* cartoon where you got extra points for being skeptical, intolerant, and otherwise oblivious. I wanted to live in a world of creativity and growth. I wanted to enjoy my life. I wanted to interact with people who brought me joy and do the same for them.

There *had* to be things that I could do for a living that would be fun and fulfilling. Great, can't wait to start! There was just one minor issue: no one was going to pay me for doing them.

Or would they?

Stand-up Comedy

I'd always had it in my mind that it would be so much fun to be a stand-up comedian. And I really thought I had the potential to do it. I was witty. I told jokes. I even gave performances. It seemed I was on my way. I was making a life, a real living, with comedy. Then the world beneath me changed and I turned seven.

It was at this tender age that I had the audacity to convey my heartfelt desire out loud: "I want to be a funny person on TV." But my second-grade teacher, Mrs. Ogden, most wise from her years of experience in the entertainment industry (aka religiously watching Archie Bunker on *All in the Family*), voiced a different opinion: "Ha! Don't be dumb. Get back in your seat." Yes, my first heckler was my second-grade teacher, who knew?

Wait a second. Did Mrs. Ogden just snatch my dream, turn it into a cherry tomato, dip it in shame, and sloppily devour it like Denethor, the steward of Gondor from *The Lord of The Rings*? Well, not exactly. Judging by her breath, not until she first marinated it in onions and garlic. What right did she have to do this? Was I *really* going to take life advice from this destroyer of children's aspirations? After all, I was a passionate dreamer with a goal. Was I going to let this fungus of a human being get in the way of my life's work?

Well . . . *yeah*! After all, she was my homeroom elementary school teacher which, to put things in perspective, is kind of like the Dalai Lama for Buddhists, the pope for Catholics, or *Duck Dynasty* for Louisianans. Credentialed, authoritative, and all-knowing, she was especially

xiii

knowledgeable when it came to things like career options and soaking in vats of anything that destroyed the ozone layer.

In spite of Mrs. Ogden's best efforts to blow out the comedian candle that burned inside of me, I never lost touch with my desire. The way I saw it, stand-up comedians were like superheroes. They spoke for truth and justice *and* they made you laugh along the way. They also didn't take any crap. Or if they did, they would somehow turn it around on stage with a witty comeback and always land on top of a crazy situation. For them it might have been days, months, or even years after that situation had transpired. People may have moved away, died, or fattened up on garlic-marinated children's dreams. But as far as we, the audience, were concerned, it was all happening real time and they had righted all the wrongs.

To me, comedians were untouchable and cool. People loved them even though they told it like it was. No, not "even though"—*because* they told it like it was. They were the epitome of being true to themselves, to their thoughts and feelings, no matter how good, bad, or ugly. They were also well equipped to handle any would-be heckler in the crowd that wanted to give them a bad time. These fast-thinking, witty, verbal superhumans had the power to transform negative into positive, mundane into funny, and the completely unidentifiable, unwanted pork scraps of life into a hot dog. Hmmm . . . pass the mustard. They were loved by all and I wanted in.

I had flirted with comedy before my current corporate dilemma. In 1998, I took a "clean comedy" class. Their biggest emphasis wasn't on being funny but on being "clean." The instructors felt that comedians too often went "below the belt" and didn't need to do that to be funny. While their aim was admirable, the result was completely ineffective like trying to convince programmers at your company that Lunchables may not be the ideal choice for a first date. I think the best joke I came up with in the class was this:

"They say the early bird gets the worm. In that case, you can have the worm. I'll sleep in and get the Quarter Pounder with Cheese."

Funny, I never did get a call from the Letterman show.

Recently I was told that a better joke might be, "They say the early bird gets the worm. In that case, you can have the worm. I'll sleep in, get an uncooked Quarter Pounder with Cheese and give myself lots of worms."

I also took a class at the San Francisco Comedy College in 2002. I really liked this class. Sure, they taught you the necessary prerequisites about comedy, but, more importantly, they taught that it had to come from an authentic place within. Comedy was about *you*. It challenged you to figure out your point of view, your perspective, your opinion on things. For a guy who had historically only offered politically correct opinions and the answers to Biff Tannen's math quiz, this was a great learning experience. Although when I think about it, how crazy is it that I needed a class to teach me how to get in touch with, embrace, and communicate my inner thoughts and feelings? I'm sure this only happens in our society. After all, you don't see lions walking around saying to their prey, "Oh no, Phil. I'm not salivating. I'm just so glad to see you that I'm crying from my mouth."

The basic comedian concepts were floated in the beginning class. That was the easy part. The next step, in the advanced class, was to actually get on stage in front of an audience, also known as "drunk people." This was terrifying to me. Me—a comedian? What will people think? I know Mrs. Ogden, for one, would definitely not approve. At the time, the thought that someone from my "normal life" might see me doing stand-up and call me out was too overwhelming—"You're not a comedian! You're responsible! Get off the stage!"

I had a professional life, or at least a veneer of one, and *that's* what was on display for the public. The freak flag had to fit nicely under the floorboards and behind the boxes labeled "Christmas 1979." And under no circumstances could it be shown to other professionals. Being on stage, I would have a lot of explaining to do, or so I thought.

Consequently, I decided to drop out. At least for the time being. Sadly, I became just another "comedy statistic."

Flash-forward to 2010, a very difficult year. In addition to being miserable at work, my nephew of eighteen years unexpectedly passed away. It was not only a stressful time but also a very sad one with little to no relief. I didn't feel I could really talk with anyone who was in the same world that I was living in. Moreover, I was the breadwinner of our family, which included two young kids and one on the way. Consequently, I felt I had to keep my "game face" on at all times. I was paranoid in the corporate environment and didn't trust it. Worse, I was working for a person who would gladly sell his mother for twenty dollars and a half-eaten quart of pork fried rice. I had to hold my feelings in. I was apprehensive of letting any emotion escape for fear that, once flowing, it wouldn't stop until I was completely deflated, wrinkled, and dried up like a tomato that's been on the vine too long, or Keith Richards.

I was ready to pop. I knew that if I didn't get some relief and couldn't be "real," bad things were going to happen. I wasn't sure where to turn. I seriously considered calling a counselor but decided against it. My health insurance was through my company and I was convinced that if I scheduled an appointment with a shrink, corporate HR's fiery-red alarm would go off, signaling there's a "freak show" in sector four. As a result, my name would be changed to "Milton" and I would be rapidly reassigned to the Stapler Department in the basement.

It was then that I turned back to comedy, not out of aspiration but desperation. My reasoning was that it was a lot less complicated than signing up for a shrink. You could tell your story, people would listen, and, best of all, there was no paperwork. On stage, I could say, "I hate my job and if I get hit by a bus today, I can miss the 10 a.m. staff meeting" and there wouldn't be someone asking annoying questions like, "Well, how does that make you feel?" and more importantly, "Did you make a backup of Biff Tannen's math quiz?"

I also had a captive audience. They weren't going anywhere, lest they lose their place in line for counseling . . . err, I mean, "performing." Sorry bastards. I kind of felt bad for them having to breathe in all of my life-drama flatulence. Then again, theirs weren't exactly bloomed roses either. The great thing was, I didn't just have one counselor; I had many. And they were all . . . listening. Moreover, I realized that other people were just as confused, bewildered, and scared as I was. I had found heaven, or at least a crazy person's wet dream, which was close enough for me.

What I found interesting was that many other comedians were just like me. They needed to get some "realness" in their life. They needed to find their voice, their authenticity. They were tired of faking their emotions at work but didn't exactly know how to act in this politically correct, "Mommy's not mad, but stop stabbing small mammals with your dinner fork" world we live in today.

I fit right into the situation. I found my voice. I made life-long friends, and have been doing comedy ever since. I have worked through many of the issues I was dealing with and it helps me continually exorcise the demons. That said, these days, I feel more aspirational about it. It helped me deal with my life situation, but it also provided me with numerous gifts that have brought me joy and have helped be more effective and fulfilled in my career and my life. So, although it inspired me, after several years of doing it, I realized that my goal was not to be a *professional* stand-up comedian. While I love being on stage and want to continue doing it, I still enjoy things like paychecks and sober people.

I also realized that I really like what I do in the business world. I found that when I brought the things that made me good at stand-up comedy into my professional business world, it freed me. It enabled me to engage as "me." It filled me with a sense of purpose and the courage to start my own business. It also made me much more effective and well, real. And if all that failed, it gave me more material to work with and an applauding confessional booth.

So now I feel I have both worlds. I have a business life that I really enjoy that supports my family. I also have the joy, connection, laughter, and fun I get from the stand-up comedy world.

And my mother always told me, "When you find something that brings you joy in this world, you have to pass it on." While I love my mom and her great advice dearly, I neither share her apparent joy of cold sores and the need to pass them on to offspring. However, I figured that, alas, there might be others who needed a little help taking out the emotional trash, finding their own voice, or just having more fun. What if the lessons I learned from living in this dual world could help them as well? Thus, the purpose of this book is to share with you those key learnings I took from stand-up comedy and applied to business in the hopes that you can use them as well. After all, comedy is no longer just for the cast of *Saturday Night Live*, illustrious dreamers, and the perpetually unemployed. Not only can it bring you joy, but it has a significant part to play in helping you do great business and live a fulfilled life.

Context and Intent

These lessons from stand-up comedy helped me find myself. They enabled me to break free of living outside of my heart and soul. They also helped me find my voice, be present, and stop doing things for reasons besides experiencing joy and fulfilment. These lessons will in turn help you say what *you* want, feel what *you* want, and do what *you* want to be the person *you* want to be—and yes, without getting fired.

For those of you terrified to do stand-up comedy or even speak in public, don't worry. While the lessons can help you in those domains, they are intended for business people who have never tried, and might never try, stand-up comedy.

You know when people use sports analogies to describe a business situation—"par for the course," "here's the game plan," or "dude, you just bit my ear off"? You clearly don't need to be good at golf, football, or cannibalism to understand and use them. Likewise, you don't need to be any kind of comedian, stand-up or otherwise, to get value from this book.

Similarly, while it can also be helpful to refer to this book if you are a stand-up comedian, it is not a "how to do stand-up 101" course. The lessons are more about finding your true voice so you can experience joy and become more fulfilled and effective in your career. A good example of this is my "Presence" chapter. While it's true that presence is a must for any good stand-up routine, I believe that it can help *anyone* with whatever they are doing. By the way, what were we talking about again?

There are many books out there on creating and delivering humor if you want to learn how to write and deliver funny. If that is your aim, I would highly recommend the San Francisco Comedy College. If not, and just to put a finer point on this, let's take it down a notch, shine the spotlight, and break out some detective cigarette smoke while we go through this just one more time. To understand and use the "golden comedic lessons" (even though they're written in black),

YOU DON'T:

- Need to be a stand-up comedian
- Need to be a wannabe stand-up comedian (that job's taken by yours truly)
- Even need to be funny. Just look at me. No, really though, trust me on this.

ADDITIONAL YOU DON'TS: (cause, yeah, I needed a word that would make me question apostrophes)

YOU DON'T:

- Need to get in front of an audience
- Need to write a bunch of knock-knock jokes Although here is one: "Knock knock? Who's there? Yah? Yahoo? Yeah, who writes knock, knock jokes anymore?"
- Need to fail in front of people. The way I see it, stand-up comedy is all about failing in front of a lot of people and, well, I've gotten really good at this! In fact, I've done enough failing for both of us, so why not just take the lessons I've learned and SUCCEED!

Finally, this book is written as if you and I already know each other and we're friends (by the way, don't you owe me twenty bucks?) or, at least, friendly acquaintances. I'll be writing as if we're sitting down for a coffee or beer and shooting the breeze. As a result, the language I use is very informal. The really good news is that I promise not to use over-engineered words to try and make myself look intelligent—you know, like *triangulate*, *robust*, and *bigly*. Oh, and there will be some profanity. If, for example, if I'm explaining a difficult situation at work, I'm not going to refer to it as an "unsavory landscape" because (1) it just sounds dumb, (2) I'm not a pompous Londoner of 1812, and (3) I've never actually tasted land. I'm getting a drink, with you, a friend, and I'm going to call it like it is: a "corporate shit-fest." If this offends you, you should immediately return this book and repent for twenty-seven days. Regardless of your denomination, that should more than clear your path to heaven. This assumes of course that you haven't been reading this in the bathroom the whole time. Then, I'm afraid this germ-infested book is yours forever. Wow, and here I thought *I* was informal.

Okay, that's enough context and disclaimers for now. For those of you who would like to learn how to experience more joy and become more fulfilled and effective in the business world and have a blast doing it, I invite you in to the world of Comediology, where you will learn the hidden secrets of stand-up comedy and how to apply them in your daily business life. For you brave souls out there, I invite you to take the blue pill. Or was it the red one? D'oh!

By the way, this book is structured so that the first section of each chapter will introduce a comedic concept and use stories and examples of my comedic experience to illustrate it. The second section of each chapter, titled *Comediology,* is about how those concepts apply to the business world.

And the good news is all you need to do is listen and (shameless ask) provide five stars on Amazon. Or...you can just send me Bitcoin, you know, provide it's worth uhhh...something.

This way . . .

Busi·ness

A person's regular occupation, profession, or trade, which, if left unchecked without fun, can lead to your soul being sucked dry and consequently morphing you into the equivalent of a stale Ritz cracker but, you know, without all the "cheddah."

Com·e·dy

The study of professional entertainment or amusement, consisting of jokes and satirical sketches, intended to make an audience laugh, and historically occupied by food service workers and the unemployed.

Com·e·di·ol·o·gy

Applying successful comedic techniques, traditionally used to amuse, entertain, or make an audience laugh, to your regular occupation, profession, or trade to enhance your daily effectiveness, fulfillment, and joy.

We are all here on Earth to help others; what on Earth the others are here for I don't know.

—*W. H. Auden*

Why Are You Here?

I've always had a passion to do stand-up comedy because I love to connect with people through laughter. I just never had the huevos—sorry, balls—to do it. Then I reached a point in my life where I officially gave up that thing that young people call "hope." I called this time of my life the "trough of disillusionment," but others might refer to it as turning forty.

It was through this phase that I really needed some help getting through the hard times. Something that would give me perspective and help me cope with life and that wasn't alcohol, drugs, gambling, a gold chain, Corvette, or anyone who called themselves "Cherry Pie."

This period forced me to look outward for a solution that would, ironically, make me look inward for perspective. This solution would not only help me survive the rough times, but also nourish the comedic fire that had been burning in me for years. The solution I found was a stand-up comedy school. The San Francisco Comedy College, to be exact, founded and operated by Kurtis Matthews, a comedian, teacher, prophet, and friend with a funny walk and too many credentials to list right now.

The college was for those interested in learning more about stand-up comedy. I couldn't believe my luck that such a thing actually existed. Thankfully, they took in overly stressed professionals and the unemployed alike. Best of all, they didn't require that you had previously graduated from comedy high school.

I learned a lot at the Comedy College. For example, I learned that my wife liked having me out of out of the house once a week. Oh yeah, I also learned the theory of humor, which, I can say wholeheartedly, did not make me funnier. Anytime I've been introduced to a "theory," it went something like this: "Blah, blah, blah—well, that's the theory anyway." It always felt like a disclaimer as to why they were going to completely mess up whatever happened next. Or, you know, die. Comedy was no exception.

And now having learned the "theory," I too was going to completely mess up whatever happened next. And boy, did I mess it up . . . theoretically.

I learned how to create material. I learned how to structure a joke. And I learned how to be nauseous and pee at least ten minutes before going on stage. I also learned how to perform. Well, I should say, I *understood* the concept of performing. With stand-up, no matter how long you've been doing it, there's always room to completely muck it up, so you are constantly in a state of refinement—tweaking this and adjusting that—to master the art form, kind of like golf or farting in public.

When you're a beginning comedian, your internal critic is overwhelmingly observant and judgmental. What you're doing is never good enough, and everything is either over the top or dumb and pales in comparison to other comedians. It's like being a guest on any political talk show:: "No Chris, let me stop you. It tells us right there in Bezerkus 24:17 exactly what funny is! It says, and I quote, Sir, 'Chaka Khan, let me rock you, let me rock you Chaka Khan.' However, that, Sir, simply did not rock my Chaka Khan and is therefore not funny, not funny at all. Sharon told a great joke, she's funny and has a lovely blouse. Joe told a spectacular joke—spectacular! He's funny and has nice jeans. You, Chris, told a crap joke; you are not funny and you are wearing dirty underwear! You are a loser! You need to go home and cry like a socialist."

As part of the class finale, we were to perform seven minutes on stage in front of a "live" audience. Well, like tank lobsters in a seafood restaurant, they were live *before* our act anyway. As you can imagine, this was a very daunting endeavor. Think about the most embarrassing thing you've ever done. Now, multiply it by seven minutes add twenty observers (some of them still awake) and bright lights pointed directly at you. Oh, and be sure to throw in a couple of "What the shiznickle was I thinking?!"s because you *volunteered* for this! Do you know how long seven minutes is on stage? Abs have been cut and defined into a perfect six-pack in less time. Death is much quicker and more painless. Even the worst sex you've ever had in your life is 6 minutes and 52 seconds shorter. I know this because I was probably there. But here I was, ready to basically lock myself into a public humiliation chamber for seven minutes. Seven #!@! minutes! What if I died? Or worse yet, lived?!

Comediology

Much of the stress came from thinking, "Who am *I* to get up in front of this audience and—okay, let's be real—*pretend* to be a comedian"? This was worse than a final exam because everyone in the room would know how I did on each answer—immediately. And they would laugh at me. Or, worse, wouldn't. I had nowhere to run, nowhere to hide and I'm pretty sure I had to pee. Moreover, I was all alone up there. It's not like I could drop the microphone, secretly peer over at the comedian sitting next to me, and be like, "hey, what's the answer to number four? Be quick, people are watching!"

It was very daunting. I needed to focus. I needed to prepare. I needed some Valium. I needed to take all the lessons I had learned over the past eight weeks and apply them—quickly. Otherwise, people were going to know I was a fake. A fraud. A hack.

The big night finally came and I was, well, freaked to the bone. I was about to get in front of drunken, raging tigers, and instead of offering them a meal, the only thing I had to fend them off was my material, which basically amounted to some skin, bones, and big '80s hair—kind of like Richard Simmons on a stick. I was rethinking the whole thing. I knew it was possible, I just didn't know if *I* could do it. I had been watching the other comedians perform and they'd made the audience laugh. They had done it. Couldn't I?

The week before my performance had been all about memorization. I told my jokes over and over in my mind and had them down pat. I also practiced the delivery repeatedly to where I had just the right incantations, inflections, and timing. I tirelessly asked my wife, "Is this one funny? Is that one funny?" I literally did this right up to the point where I got up on stage. No, I mean literally. I was asking people for feedback *minutes* before my performance. After numerous iterations, however, people were like, "Dude, I can't listen to your bullshit again." In her defense, that Walmart greeter was having a rough day.

I was finally introduced by the host and I started walking up on stage. I saw things in tunnel vision. The last thought I had before grabbing the microphone was, "Dear God, please don't let me forget my material. In return, I promise to never carelessly put my used Dixie cup in the compost bin again . . . errr, unless that's the bin it goes in, and—oh yeah, that whole impure thoughts thing, ugh, never mind."

I stepped up on stage and shook the host's hand. At least I hoped it was his hand. One of the first things you notice while being on stage is the lights. They are overwhelmingly bright and they shine directly on you. Apparently, lots of light is needed during deliveries, whether that delivery is a baby or comedy. Akin to prison, it also serves as a reminder—"Z'er is no iscape . . . Mwahahahah!" Oh, and now you know why Donald Trump is orange.

I grabbed the microphone and started talking. I could hear my voice start to crackle and shrink like MC Hammer in 1992 (feel free to look him up). I was completely focused on my material and presented it just as I practiced. It was very similar to my rehearsals. In fact, the only real differences that I noticed was that it was ten times faster, had no pauses, and, oh yeah, wasn't funny. The imaginary audience I had prepared with were so much more appreciative and in tune with good comedy than this bunch of hostages. As a result, I received the worst sound ever. The same sound I got when I professed my feelings of true love to Jenny in middle school—silence. Well, almost. At least in Jenny's case, she had the decency to return from staring off into space with a "Hmmm . . . hey, you got mustard on your chin."

After I was done with my verbal spewing, I walked down off the stage and quickly looked for a place to hide, like a bathroom stall or Inner Mongolia. I couldn't go too far, though. I had brought friends and family to the event, so I had to make a reappearance after the show. Once reunited with them, I didn't say much and neither did they. I was embarrassed, and they were embarrassed for me, which is way worse than just being embarrassed by yourself. Misery loves company. Embarrassment, on the other hand, just isn't ready for a relationship right now. The only thing worse than the silence was the consolation, "Hey, at least you tried really hard." Which is kind of like saying, "Wow, you really sucked balls up there, but you had sweat rings so we could tell you wanted to do better." I was kind of hoping someone from the audience would walk up, put their arm around me, and say "Well, at least you don't have Ebola." It would have hurt but it would have been a funnier thing to put in a book than what had actually happened.

I went home and swore I would never do comedy again. Actually, they were two separate events. First I swore, *then* I swore I would never

Comediology

do comedy again. I know, it's a lot of swearing (sorry gals, I'm taken). But stand-up is one of those things you *have* to do. Otherwise, why would anyone do it in the first place? For whatever reason, we comedians choose to put ourselves in a situation where people judge us, and often we fail. Maybe we are reincarnated souls from the Salem witch-burning era and apparently just can't get enough of the good ol' days.

This went on for several of my sets. After many silent audiences later, my instructor Kurtis asked me a simple question: "Chris, why are you doing this?"

Although thought provoking, this question was decidedly *not* a confidence booster. I responded, "Well, I just want to have fun and connect with people."

He responded, "Then why aren't you doing that?"

My first inclination was to get defensive: "But . . . wait, you told me to follow the joke theory! And . . . I shared each and every one of my jokes with you before I told them onstage and embarrassed myself. Why didn't you say anything then?! This is all your fault! You made me look like a fool! I'll never get back to Kansas now, never!"

Yes, I let my "victim" have his day in the sun. I call him "Vic." He's angry with you. He's angry with everyone. "*How could you do this to him?!* What's that? You don't even know him? Well then, *how could you abandon him like this?!* Oh, you were with him all along? Well, then quit limiting his potential!" He could do this all day long. . . .

After many Wayne Dyer books later, I finally realized Kurtis was right. I had been so focused on the mechanics of joke telling, or the *what*, I had forgotten *why* I was there in the first place. Getting on stage wasn't fun for me. In fact, it was a terrifying and horrific experience. I realized I wasn't allowing myself the freedom to be me. I had limited my abilities to a joke-telling methodology. Moreover, I had measured success by comparing myself to others. This type of comparison was never good for my ego in the gym locker room, so why would it be any different now? Oh, and just for the record, on senior citizen discount day, I am the undisputed king.

And where was I in all this equation? I was a watered-down version of myself. I had given up all my spunk, spark, and passion for guides and judgment that were completely outside of me. But what about my joy? My

5

Chris S. Tabish with Kurtis Matthews

direction? And my "why"—the whole reason I was up there in the first place?

Could I change the rules?

I had to rethink this. No, I had to *re-feel* this. It sounded crazy and a little bit scary to deviate from the methodology used by the "pros," but I needed to change it up. I truly believed I had the funny within me. Besides, how much worse could it get? I mean, really. My act was about as funny as a dead canary floating atop a bowl of tomato soup.

I decided to change three things. First, I decided to be present and have fun. No matter what happened, I was going to find joy being on stage. If I hit it out of the park, of course it would be fun. But even if I bombed, I would still find the joy.

How could I do this? Actually, this part was simple. You see, probably just like everyone else, when I experience funny, I both think *and feel* the humor at the same time. It brings me joy inside and makes me laugh and want to share it. This I do naturally, so bringing it to the stage was a no-brainer.

So why wasn't I doing this all the time? For some reason, I erroneously traded in the thought and feeling of funny for a joke framework. It was like trying to make people laugh while trapped inside an aquarium. Furiously pounding on the glass, I would yell at the top of my voice trying to win them over. "I'm funny! Can't you people see that?! Why aren't you laughing?! Wait, don't look at him, he's a lobster! I'm way funnier than a shellfish!" But to no avail. Uninterested and perhaps a little confused, they would pass on by, commenting, "Well, the steaks are good here anyway."

I don't know if you've ever been figuratively bested by a caged crustacean. But I can tell you, it makes you really take a good look at your life. Put simply, I changed my approach immediately. And the interesting thing is, it didn't take a lot of work. All I really had to do was just be the way I normally would be. I simply brought my comedic flow to the stage—thinking, feeling, and speaking the funny that naturally comes from within me. That, and I left the hairpiece at home. Regardless of the words, I would tap into the essence of the funny. Why did I decide to bring a particular joke up? Oh yeah, 'cause it makes me laugh and I can't wait to share it with other people!

As with most other things in life, we make it overly complex and difficult on ourselves. Yet it's really quite simple. Yes, you do need a plan. That said, there was once a famous philosopher from 1980s, by the name of Mike Tyson, who brilliantly stated, "Everyone's got a plan until they get punched in the mouth." This is why you need to go back to *being you, but, you know,* without ever biting another guys ear off. All you really need is your heart, your passion, your soul, your presence, and your "why," and the Force will be with you . . . *always.*

Comediology

This was my journey in comedy, but it happens constantly to us in the business world, too. For example, have you ever had a strong passion or "why" to do something? Perhaps you wanted to entertain people, or help the underprivileged, or build great things that would inspire generations. However, you didn't have the credentials, education, money, or naked pictures of the governor to achieve it. Yeah, me neither. It was very discouraging. From there, you probably did one of two things. Option one is you gave up on your dream and decided henceforth, you will no longer be Superman, the Incredible Hulk, or Batman. (Bruce Wayne, however, was still an option to be considered.)

Option two is you went out and got a lot of "what"s to help you make your dream come true. You wanted to be the biggest, brightest, and best and, to do that, you concluded, you needed some "what"s—money, education, a methodology, or a marriage proposal from Roseanne Barr. You invested a lot of yourself in acquiring these, too. And it took time. Perhaps you spent years of your life acquiring these "what"s to help realize your dream.

Along your journey, you took note of other people's paths as well. You saw what they received along the way. You started comparing your "what"s to theirs, and sometimes, your "what" looked bigger and better, but sometimes it didn't. You felt a tinge of bitterness swell inside of you when you saw this disparity. You may have even emulated others to achieve similar "what"s It seemed like the journey had shifted from "living the why" to "getting the what." As a result, you found yourself unfulfilled and very lost. You asked yourself some very important questions: Why am I

Chris S. Tabish with Kurtis Matthews

doing this? What do I get from these "what"s? And why does my life sound like a Dr. Seuss story?

Then you bumped into someone who was, well, different. They had passion in their eyes, intention in their movements, and yet carried no incriminating pictures. Everything they did and said seemed to resonate truth. The funny thing was, they weren't focused on the "what"s. As a matter of fact, they didn't even care what people thought of them, star on their belly or not. They were focused on the "why." And, more specifically, *their* "why." They were committed to doing this while letting the chips fall as they may. It was like living the "why" was their intrinsic reward and they didn't give a hoot about the "what"s. This of course made you first question all the money you'd been spending on belly stars. And then inquire, WHY AM I DOING THIS?!

But alas, you, too, realized the secret. Shhhh!!! You want to give it away?! Hold on. We should put it in a book and sell it! Oh wait, this *is* the book. Sorry . . . never mind.

Contrary to our popular societal belief, *you don't need a "what" to add value or achieve your dreams.*

We can clearly see this as it pertains to our dreams, but even in everyday life, we focus on the "what" and the "how," when we're not even clear on the "why."

We see this all the time. "We need to implement this new software as soon as possible!" Okay, but *why*? Is it to make salespeople in our company more productive, give our customers a better experience, or was it just a weak moment when you just needed the person selling you the software to not talk anymore?

It is *paramount* to understand and articulate the "why" to everyone. Make it abundantly clear for you and them. The "why" will affect your day-to-day approach as well as the success of any initiative, and people can immediately and constantly add value because *they* get it. Why is it that the value from most efforts is deferred until a project "goes live"? This seems so crazy to me. For example, if the "why" was to make salespeople's lives more productive, why can't you start helping them—*right now*?

For example, you could share the customer data you've gathered to date, or the ways they can make the quote process more efficient. You could also share the formatting shortcut that can shave minutes off each

Comediology

of their proposals and that hard-to-reach place under the nostrils. Some of these can all help them *right now* and it's perfectly aligned with the "why."

Even if you're not adding value yet, by knowing the "why," you can at least not make things worse, which, if you squint, *is* adding value. For example, you could be more efficient and condense that two-hour time-suck meeting to thirty minutes or a quick conversation or, better yet, a sweet, seven-word note written in permanent marker on the computer screen of your coworker. Best of all, by articulating the "why," you get people to start thinking on how they can deliver *their value* to meet the objective. They will be using their originality, their creativity, their life essence to meet the "why." Contrast this to being stuck in following the corporate methodology of doing a "what" or "how."

One of my favorite examples of this dates back to 1962. President John F. Kennedy was touring the NASA space center when he came across a janitor. Interrupting his tour, he went over to the man and said, "Where the hell is your green card?" Sorry, I'm getting my administrations confused. What he actually said was "Hi, I'm Jack Kennedy. What are you doing?"

"Well, Mr. President," the janitor replied, "I'm helping put a man on the moon."

I get inspired just by listening to this response. This man was living a very powerful "why." It's motivational, inspiring, and fulfilling. And yes, "I'm helping put a man on the moon" will produce far superior results than, "Oh, yeah, who left the iron-rich meteorite in the commode module?"

The "what"s rarely provide us long-term value, joy, fulfillment, or even accomplishment. Your "why," however, *is* special. It *does* do those things. It's unique. And in my experience, this is what people are really after. Just look at any advertisement. The "what's" are everywhere and they are *commonplace*. You compare them feature by feature because, let's face it, they're really not that much different from one another. Occasionally, however, we uncover a product, person, place, or thing that *is* really different. It is special. It is unique. We see its "why" shining through and it easily surpasses all of the heartless "what"s, not feature by feature, but by heart and soul.

For example, when you purchase Apple products, do you really do a feature-to-feature comparison—hard drive space, screen resolution, and the like? In my experience, no. You purchase them because they're beautiful, amazing, head-turning products based upon the "why" of their co-founder, Steve Jobs, who was exposed to, and passionate about, the art of calligraphy. As he described it, "I learned about serif and sans-serif typefaces, about varying the amount of space between different letter combinations, about what makes great typography great. It was beautiful, historical, artistically subtle in a way that science can't capture, and I found it fascinating. None of this had even a hope of any practical application in my life. But 10 years later, when we were designing the first Macintosh computer, it all came back to me. And we designed it all into the Mac."

Just think, if only Steve Jobs had stayed a "what." If he had just followed the common practices and methodologies of design, we would have ourselves another "c-o-m-p-u-t-e-r." BOOOOOOORRRRRIIIINNNGGG! Thank goodness he didn't limit himself to the "what" but, instead, got in touch with his "why" and trusted in it to the point of its driving the manifestation of his creation. We see that beauty, that refinement, that "wow" factor in his products even today, years after his death.

I didn't need any material or methodology to connect with people and have fun. For me, it's like breathing. But somehow, I didn't do this in comedy. I saw a label like "stand-up comedy" and it became daunting and somehow completely outside of me and my abilities. I saw it as something that was external, something that I needed to adjust myself to *attain* rather than something inside of me that was both unique and special that I could *give*. I now believe that I was drawn to stand-up comedy in the first place *because* I had that passion inside of me that needed to be released, and this was the catalyst to enable it. In fact, my best moments on stage were not from my material and most certainly not from the methodology. They were extemporaneous and stemmed from living my "why"—connecting with people through laughter. *I* brought this. My natural desires, passions, and abilities shined through and it was pure bliss.

I'm not saying methodologies, degrees, diplomas, and the like aren't useful. At my dentist's office, for example, they really stand out as not being yet another picture of someone with better teeth than me. And I am really grateful that my doctor learned how to do surgery instead of just serendipitously appearing before me with a scalpel, a curious mind, and a Freddy Krueger grin. That said, I'm even more grateful for my doctor's "why." Without his even saying so, I knew he was there to help me and would do whatever it took to get what I needed. Without this, a degree, methodology, or procedure would be useless, or downright scary. As a result, you would receive a painful procedure, an everlasting cavity, or a supporting role in a *Duck Dynasty* episode

You've got a passion inside of you. Perhaps you've just forgotten about it, or never realized it, but *it's in there.* Somewhere beneath all of the methods, degrees, and pressure to be Oprah with Kim Kardashian's curves (sorry, not you, Hank), there it is: your spunk, your passion, your underlying reason for saying yes to whatever it is you need to do in your life.

The way I see it, bringing your "why" is like travelling to a destination via airplane. In this analogy, you are your "why" and your luggage is your "what." Here's what happens. The plane lands, the doors open, and you step out into the new world and start making your way. Alas, you find yourself in the baggage claim area and you see your luggage—your "what"—coming around the bend. This luggage will help you function in your new destination. It will provide clothing, toiletries, and by the looks of them, slightly infected Q-tips from the previous trip. These things, of course, will assist you in your new destination.

What's that, you say? Your luggage didn't arrive? Well, that clearly is a sign that you need to put your tail between your legs (okay, yes, you're right—grow one first), then turn around and get on the next flight back home. Who were you to think you could travel to a new destination? You clearly come from a "one-destination" lineage and those folks at Delta will see to it that people are appropriately put away in the right "life bin." After all, your great-grandfather never carelessly hopped on a flying machine risking lost luggage, broken dreams, and airplane flatulence just so that he could "explore a new world." And he did just "fine" at the buttermilk factory.

Okay, what?! No! Everyone knows you don't turn around and return to your destination just because you forgot your handlebar moustache glue. And don't quote me on this, but I'm confident they'll still be selling Preparation H and toenail clippers at your new destination. You stay at your destination and you figure it out because luggage (aka your "what") is nice to have, but your "why," the reason for you being there, is *critical*. Are you interviewing for a new job? Are you there to meet family or perhaps a romantic interest? Maybe you're on a vacation or even a honeymoon?

Whatever the reason, you're going to go do it, and it will influence *everything* you do, regardless of your luggage or lack thereof. It's easy to realize this when we're talking about lost luggage, but somehow we lose sight of this in our own lives.

I think one of the reasons we so easily lose sight of the "why" is because our language speaks in "what"s and completely bypasses the "why"s. For example, we say, "I want to be an accountant." But if we explored the "why," we might realize what we really mean is, "Numbers fascinate me and I love helping people with finances." We say, "I want a new job," but what when we might really mean is, "I want to work at a place with 'my kind of people' and make a positive difference in the world." We say, "I want to find an attractive boyfriend," when we really mean, "In your face, high school reunion!"

Why do we speak in "what"s and not "why"s? I'm not sure exactly. Perhaps we do it because it's a defense mechanism that protects us from feeling too much. Then again, maybe it's because speaking in "why's" would simply require too much time. Imagine the guy in front of you on the restaurant line professing his adulation of lunging weasels when you're like, "Dude, just order the vegetarian omelet already!" Or, perhaps it's for a much more basic reason. You know, maybe we're just dumb.

Regardless of the reason, remember that the "what's" are a means to an end, not the end within itself. Your true fulfillment and joy lies within the "why." Trying to find it in the "what" is as imposturous as that furry, unnatural orange creature on Donald Trump's head trying to pass itself off as hair.

Why are you doing what you are doing? **This simple answer is paramount.** *Never underestimate it. This is your north star. This will guide you through every twist and turn in your life. Once you **live** your "why" and stop trying to fit into somebody else's "what" or "how," you will thrive with internal fulfillment and you will kick ass on **your** stage, whatever that may be.*

Comediology

Summary

For those of you who can't be bothered with the details and just quickly need the answers to Monday's 9 a.m. math quiz, here goes...

1) **Get in touch with your "why."**

   What drives you? What are you passionate about? Try to understand the underlying reason you are doing the activity for which you are engaged.

2) **Feel the joy of pursuing your "why," regardless of the outcome.**

   Let the "what's" fall where they may. Pursuing our "why" brings us joy and fulfillment.

3) **Measure success by what *you* can control**. If you are truly pursuing your "why," you are being courageous, you are having fun, and you are living your purpose. You are a success. Period.

4) **Yes, even if it seems useless now, pursue your passion—you never know**. As it turns out for all iPhone users, calligraphy was useful. Who knew? Instead of thinking about what you are *getting*, pursue your why, feel the joy, and think about what you are *becoming*.

The duty of comedy is to correct men by amusing them.

—Moliere

Why Comedy?

We pay good money to see stand-up shows and funny movies. We get addicted to our favorite sitcoms. We quote the funniest lines over and over again. We tell jokes. We laugh. We love comedy. But why?

I think one of the reasons I love comedy so much is that it positively connects people. I see it just about every time I watch my six-year-old, Charlie, interact with his best friend, Mitch. Now, as I said, they are *best friends*. However, about once every, say, oh I don't know, FIVE MINUTES, they end up in some sort of argument that they can't seem to work past. It could be something as minuscule as Charlie taking the bat when clearly it was Mitch's turn to hit the ball, or Mitch not wanting to play the game that Charlie has suggested. Alternatively, it could be something very important, like Charlie firmly believing that he is wearing superior underwear compared to Mitch's. Whatever it is, ultimately this disagreement spirals into a standoff where Charlie and Mitch end up on opposite ends of the room with folded arms and pouty faces, each looking like a victim of a heinous crime or John McEnroe.

I see this and immediately demand that both of them come to the center of the room. From here, I tell them, "This looks bad, you guys. It looks like this might be the end for you two. We're going to have to see if, in fact, you guys are true friends or not. The only way to do this, of course, is to take the friendship test."

The friendship test goes like this. Mitch and Charlie are instructed to stare into each other's eyes for thirty seconds. If neither of them cracks a smile during this time, then, alas, they are no longer friends. However, if either does smile or laugh, then they are, in fact, true friends and need to go back to playing right away.

Both Mitch and Charlie agree and start this "scientifically proven" test. It is, of course, neither scientific nor proven, but something that I completely made up. It is a total farce and has no technical credentials

Chris S. Tabish with Kurtis Matthews

whatsoever. That said, I saw it being touted as "credible evidence" on Fox News just the other day.

The test starts and the tension is thick. Both Mitch and Charlie stare into each other's eyes with anger and hurt. *"Ready,"* I say, *"get set you guys. . . . "* At this moment, the fury immediately dissipates and it's abundantly clear they can't do it. As much as they try to hold it in, the laughter is too much to bear. They want to hold on to their anger but one of them smiles and it fractures their armor. Then, seeing the other one smile and crack under the pressure, they both go into a full-blown belly laugh. It is over before it even began and, to this day, they're still best friends.

For me, comedy is like this. It's *real*. For something to be funny and make us laugh, it usually has to bring out the essence of truth. In Charlie and Mitch's case, the truth is that in spite of any short-term disagreement, they really do enjoy each other and are best friends—and also they're both being *ridiculous*. It can be observational, self-evident, or confessional, but the *real truth* shines out. This is one of the reasons I think comedy resonates with us. In a funny and entertaining way, it calls it like it is. This does many things for our spirit. First, it is our ticket to the lighter side of life. Second, it enables open and honest communication. Last, it produces laughter, which has numerous health benefits.

Comedy Is Our Ticket to the Lighter Side of Life

Comedy helps us resolve situations that are otherwise embarrassing, traumatic, scary, distasteful, or, worst of all, boring. This resolution usually occurs after the fact, upon reflection. Yet it can also resolve things in real time. It's comedy, for example, that helps me persevere every time I get on the golf course.

Wente Vineyards, Livermore, California. It's a beautiful, sunny day and I'm out on the golf course with my friends. I'm dressed in all the right gear—new golf shoes, glove, and visor. Oh yeah, and I have not the first clue as to what I'm doing. Contrary to how I'm dressed, I'm a *total* hack. It's a good thing I am quite skilled at laughing at myself or I would definitely be too critical, embarrassed, or self-conscious to get out here.

Our tee time arrives and the teacher from Charlie Brown announces our name on the loudspeaker. "Waaa waaaa mmeee waa mee waaa

Comediology

foursome on tee number one." Sure, got it. With standers-by and my fellow golf mates watching.

I tee off. Why is it so quiet? Could one of you at least have the courtesy to talk during by backswing so I could blame this crappy shot on you? Hmmm . . . no dice. I pretend to warm up. I even throw in a grunt or two just to corroborate my golfing intensity, 'cause apparently I'm cool like that.

I lift my club and go into my backswing. With a mighty Thor-like stroke, I bring down the hammer. Down it comes—whack! I hit the ball and it goes. It's going—somewhere. Yes, it is. It is going somewhere! Whoo-hoo! I have made contact with the ball and in fact, the ball is going somewhere!

No. No, wait a second, I spoke too soon. It's going "somewhere. Somewhere—*else.*" Ooooh, now that's interesting. It's on the other fairway. In fact, it's making its way toward the fairway opposite from the one I'm on. Wow, I've outdone myself and achieved a new level of embarrassment.

Wait . . . it's not just embarrassing. Look at those golfers on the other fairway. I'd better warn them. "Fore!!!" I yell. I can see their body language as the ball whizzes by them. They're not happy. In fact, they're downright pissed off. They give me some serious stank-eye. I imagine what they're saying, "Get out of the way, Chuck, this guy's !#@!@ crazy! What the hell is he doing on the course, anyway?!" "What a jackass!"

Obviously, they were never a "beginner." That's it. Based on this behavior, I've decided that I'm not inviting them to golf on the opposite fairway from me next year and that's final. Yes, I nearly hit them with the ball, but they are being total jerks. They deserve to be shaken up a bit. To that point, I've changed my mind. I'm *definitely* inviting them to golf on the opposite fairway from me next year, and *that's* final.

It's funny—everyone was completely silent on the backswing, but somehow, it got eerily quieter. On one hand, the sting is overwhelming. My green, cow fart of a hit is in public and it stinks really, *really* bad. There are witnesses! It's so bad, no one even wants to laugh—"Yes, Alex, I'll take 'Awkward Moments' for a thousand." With the uncomfortable glances of onlookers and a deafening quiet within my foursome, it makes me want to curl up into a fetal ball.

Things are seemingly at their worst. But it is at *exactly* this point where the magic happens. This is where the comedy kicks in. Maybe it's because those guys are jerks, maybe it's because I'm a jerk, too, but I can't help myself—I feel the funny bubbling up inside of me.

I say to my friends, "Isn't this great? I mean, what other time could I legally launch rapidly moving projectiles at pretentious strangers and pretend they're my boss? Why else would those nice people at the registration desk hand me a club and a bunch of balls with no legal waivers? Usually I have to pay for entertainment like this!"

"And for future reference," I continue, "don't waste your time in court battling the big oil companies when you can simply send me out there to find 'the man' in his natural golfing habitat—unprotected and vulnerable."

I hear a laugh. Then another. Everyone joins in and we're all laughing together. I've openly acknowledged and vocalized the "truth" about my golf game. Admittedly, my golf game is not an "Olympian's" version of golf. *My* golf game is the "Snoopy Toothbrush" version of golf. As a result of this acknowledgment, the "truth" is out there for everyone to see, and it's hysterical! What's more is that it's no longer a moment of uncomfortable embarrassment, but has transformed into a moment of shared joy and laughter.

Yes, I still suck at golf and continue to advertise that fact very visibly. Yes, it's still embarrassing. I'm not out there to hit bad shots and be humiliated, and I'm certainly not out there to hurt anybody. That said, *it is the reality* of the situation. Remember, comedy starts from a place of truth. *This* truth is the one we're all living *right now*. A friend once told me that for something to be "real," it's got to have the good, the bad, and the ugly. *Owning* the good is easy enough. But *own* the bad and the ugly, too. It's not what you aspire for, it's not what you hope for, it's "what it is, *right now*." So why not own it? Everyone else assumes you already do anyway. So, take the keys to that rusty, orange 1968 Ford Pinto and drive, man, drive! Look on the humorous side of it, let the comedy flow, laugh, and enjoy life. Don't bury the truth. Set it free and let comedy be your ally.

Comedy Enables Open and Honest Communication

Santa Clara, California. I was pulling out of a parking lot where I had stopped for coffee and was on my way to my next destination. I was running late and was therefore stressed out and in a hurry. Pulling out of

Comediology

the lot, I looked both ways, or so I thought, and then hit the gas pedal. As I entered the far lane, there was this large, annoying, white object that seemingly came out of nowhere. I had to swerve to avoid hitting it. "What a dillrod!" I said, annoyed and angry. That is until I realized that this "thing" was known in these parts as a "police car." Regardless, I didn't take kindly to this interruption and moments later, I had that bothersome police officer right where I wanted him—standing outside of my window with his ticket book in hand.

"Do you know why I pulled you over?" he asked impatiently.

To this, I immediately thought, "You were on the fairway in Livermore?" I then responded, "Can I assume it's because I'm the only one on the planet dumb enough to try and hit a police car?"

He paused. He took a step back from the car. He tried to hold it in but couldn't help himself. He started to giggle. He put his hand on the car to support himself and started laughing. Then I started laughing. We were both hopelessly lost in a weird, wonderful, and, yes, a bit awkward moment of hilarity. Our anger and fear both melted in the light of this laughter.

After the moment subsided, he asked me what had happened. Only this time it was different. He wasn't being "dad" inquiring why the lawn hadn't been mowed and the dog impregnated. No. This was a question of genuine concern, like, "Hey, are you sure everything is okay?" I told him everything—where I was going, why it was important, why I was late—every detail. He listened to it all. I apologized for running him off the road and he said not to worry about it. Before he sent me off, I thanked him and he told me to slow down and be safe. We shook hands briefly and then he walked back to his car. No ticket, no hassle, nothing. The whole experience was amazing and wouldn't have been possible without the magic of comedy. And for those *Reno 911!* fans, no, we didn't make out on the side of the road, which was a shame since my lips on that day were quite supple.

Without that initial bubbling up of funny, the officer wouldn't have been sympathetic or empathetic. And without that, I wouldn't have felt comfortable sharing my situation openly and honestly. Comedy built this emotional connection. It's like building a portal to another human. Instead of tapping into their judgmental cerebral cortex, however, you actually link directly to their limbic system, the emotional part of the

Chris S. Tabish with Kurtis Matthews

brain. Humor erodes the veil of judgment and connects you and your audience emotionally. Want to see this in real time? Consider these two statements.

Example "Uno." Told from "Doug," a fictitious "bad example" guy:

Doug's statement: "I believe I would be a bad father. I have fear as it pertains to dark places. This is not ideal and it would prevent me assisting others needing help while in the dark, including children."

What did you think about Doug? What a lunging weasel, right? He can't help his children in the dark? What kind of father—no, what kind of *person* is he? Are you kidding me?

Did you find yourself judging Doug? Yes, my cerebral cortex went into full scrutiny mode. (Oh yeah, do you like it when I try to sound all technical with brain parts? Yeah, me too. "Brain stem"—boom shaka laka!) So, if you are like me, Doug is a disappointment to say the least—selfish, cowardly, and just eeewwwww. Right? I picture Doug as a hunching and profusely sweating overweight guy with a '70s moustache, mullet, and moist handshake who smells like he just bathed in the sink at a rest stop.

What happened? He came to us with a confession. He was open. He was courageous in coming out to say what he said. But we still judged him, or *you* judged him anyway—*how dare you*?! He never made it past our judgment. After all, why would you take a guy like Doug in? We couldn't sympathize, couldn't empathize, couldn't relate, and certainly couldn't and wouldn't want to emotionally connect. With a moist handshake? Eeeeeewwwwww.

Now let's move on to our next example.

Example "Dos." Told by comedian Preston Tompkins.

Preston's statement: "I'd be a horrible father. Mainly because I'm still afraid of the dark. You can't be a good dad if you're afraid of the dark. If my daughter yelled, "Daaaaaaad, there's a monster under my bed!" I'd say, "Shut the fuck up, he can hear you!"

In this example, we see the same issue with one key difference—that dude is *funny*! What kind of effect did it have on you? For me, even though Preston has an obvious issue, something about it is very endearing. We definitely see the same dysfunction that Doug has. This time, however, our cerebral cortex, or "analytical" brain, is bypassed and our limbic or "emotional" brain is engaged. We care for Preston. We see the challenge from his perspective and we're on his side. There's just something about him. We see he acknowledges the issue. He doesn't take himself too seriously in the process and he is able to joke about it. It has a charming effect on us.

It's a bit crazy when you think about it. The guy is swearing at his daughter and there's something lovable about it! Okay, yes, in the real world, we would probably assume that this is a tall tale and that Preston wouldn't really swear at his daughter. But that's just it: Doug, our "bad example guy," appears to live in a state of fear, taking himself and his situation too seriously. Preston, on the other hand, has worked through his fear. He sees the ridiculousness of it all. He can make light of it and even make fun of himself in the process.

As humans, coming out and exposing our underbelly is not an easy thing to do. And with anything, there are degrees to which we do this. Doug's degree of vulnerability allowed him to at least openly acknowledge his issue. People often can't even get to that point. So let's at least get him a *Family Feud* board game as a consolation prize before sending him home. But Preston took it further. By incorporating humor, he not only acknowledged the issue and exposed his vulnerability, but he also acknowledged the absurdity of it all. In that moment, he basically told us how silly he realizes he is and how ludicrous the situation is. He *really* gets it. And because he gets it, we get him. Got it? Good.

With Preston, we see that he knows how to appropriately appraise a situation, whereas with Doug, we're not sure. To his credit, we see that he realizes he's not fit to be a good dad. But does he also realize how being perceived as "crazy" and "moist" is crashing his party of life?

There's a self-deprecating element to laughing at yourself that says, "Hey, I don't take myself so seriously that I can't have a good laugh at my own expense." Wow! We love that. We respect that. We don't see this as a lacking confidence, either. In fact, it's quite the opposite. People who declare this *are* confident in themselves, so they *can* be vulnerable. They can laugh at themselves and have others laugh at their situation as well.

He's giving us a portal. In that quick, funny story, he's told us so many things that Doug hasn't. In addition to being confident, he's communicated that he's fun. He's showed us that he's witty. He's demonstrated that he has a great imagination. He's told us that he doesn't judge himself too harshly.

Chris S. Tabish with Kurtis Matthews

Moreover, we get the impression that, if we were Preston's friend, he wouldn't judge us. He would understand we're only human and he would cut us a break as well. What's more, we would have fun together, too.

Oh yeah, and it's not just us. According to a study conducted by Seattle University, Queens University, and the University of Manitoba, leaders who use self-deprecating humor are perceived to be more caring, trustworthy and, not surprisingly, more likeable. So, fess up to those hairy troll feet or whatever *you think* you've got hidden under the hood. Bottled up, it's a burden, but belted out and rightly made fun of, it's a gift.

Comedy Gets Us Laughing. Together.

Because I do stand-up comedy as a hobby, I have the good fortune of seeing many comedians. Inevitably, I'll hear an extremely funny line from a comedian. Just the other night, in fact, I heard a brilliant joke from comedian Red Scott. It went something like this:

"I just got back from seeing the famous painting, the *Mona Lisa*. Mona Lisa is, of course, famous for her smile.

"But I have to tell you, *she's not smiling*!

"Seriously, anyone who *thinks* she's smiling is in for a life full of restraining orders."

I think that joke is hysterical. When I hear something funny like that, the first thing I want to do is share it with my friends—not the ones with restraining orders, mind you. Usually by the time I'm able to do so, I've thought about it numerous times in my head. But interestingly, it's only when I actually share the joke *out loud with others* that I physically laugh at it again.

I've often wondered about this because sometimes I think it would be so great if we could just perform *and enjoy* our stand-up routine in our own minds. We would be both comedian and audience. Think about the money we would save on overpriced parking and watered-down gin and tonics! On second thought, it would be weird telling people how amazing we performed the night previous. "If you could have only seen me on stage! I'm telling you, I was simply brilliant. My hypothalamus went absolutely crazy and demanded more. More! I didn't get to bed until 2 a.m. Five stars and kudos to me!"

Comediology

Hmmm. . . . Okay, so, thankfully it doesn't work that way. Laughter, it seems, is elusive and magically appears as a gift when we are enjoying comedy with other people. In fact, Dr. Robert Provine, a Neuroscientist and Professor of Psychology at the University of Maryland, found that we're *thirty times more likely* to laugh being with others versus being alone. Okay, well, except for Billy, the creepy giggler with no pants sitting next to you on the subway at 11 p.m. He's the noteworthy exception. He was giddy with laughter before you arrived and he'll be giddy with laughter after a face full of bear spray.

Being in touch with the funny puts us in touch with our friends, family, and everyone else in the world who also enjoys a good laugh. This is an activity best shared together. Yet while it's evidently entertaining to the individual, laughing too much on your own is, well, just weird. And, as Emperor Palpatine has demonstrated, it's clearly a one-way ticket to the dark side, not to mention bad skin, premature wrinkling, and aimlessly wandering around in your bathrobe. Yes, Yoda always laughed at his own stuff, too, but for reasons we could understand—Luke, a Jedi? Ha, right . . . that's a good one. The dude made out with his sister!

Bottom line: If you're laughing, you're probably doing it with other people. In other words, you're not bitterly enumerating the reasons why those "sons 'a bitches" are ruining the world. And that's a really good thing.

Comedy Does Wonders for Our Health

I think we all can agree that laughing is fun. Who doesn't like to laugh? But did you also know that it's really good for you? It is. Humor can alleviate depression and boost your immunity, reduces stress, lower blood pressure, and stimulate your mind. And that's if you're already dead. Just imagine if you're still alive! What's more, in many cases, your body responds positively just by *anticipating* it. That's right, *anticipating,* not actually experiencing it.

I perform stand-up comedy about once a week. It's an interesting phenomenon, too, because just *knowing* that I'm going to perform and listen to comedy puts me in a great mood. As it turns out, it's not just me; there's science behind it. Dr. Lee Berk of Loma Linda University found that in people who simply anticipated humor, beta-endorphins, which help alleviate depression, increased by 27 percent, and human growth hormone,

Chris S. Tabish with Kurtis Matthews

which helps immunity, and can also spontaneously transform you into Andre The Giant, increased by 87 percent. Likewise, cortisol, also known as the stress hormone (*now* you know who to blame), was also reduced with the same anticipation.

Did you catch that? They didn't perceive *any* humor, they just *anticipated* it. This is amazing! Just like your former boss or anyone who calls themselves "the man," you don't have to actually deliver any value, you just need to look the part. Yes, there is still one area where you can overpromise and under-deliver yet still achieve. It's called comedy.

How can you mend a broken heart Al Green? Well, for starters, probably not with that song. But perhaps comedy can help. In 2011, researchers from Oxford University discovered that people who laughed more *now* felt less pain *later*. Yes, watching or partaking in comedy led to a higher pain tolerance. Apparently, comedy is a time-release drug and, as an added bonus, doesn't cause dizziness, nausea, or anal leakage. I'm ready now—come at me bro. Oh, I still wouldn't recommend coffee and fiber bars before Chris Rock.

Comparing this to other forms of intake, we see the obvious contrast. Alcohol, for example, is classified as a depressant. But anyone who thinks that has obviously never had a tequila shot while playing "Get Down Tonight" by KC and the Sunshine Band. Regardless, with this drug and others like it, you feel the positive effects immediately. The next morning, however, when you wake up to discover that, consistent with urban legend, your American Express Card really does have no limit, you realize the down side. Not that a pet llama isn't a complete loss, mind you.

On the other hand, health food, such as broccoli and cauliflower, doesn't taste nearly as good as that cheeseburger with garlic fries. When you eat it, however, you're bound to feel positive effects, you know, like six to nine months later. You'll be walking around thinking, "Wow, I feel great. I'll bet it's because of that asparagus I ate last December."

With comedy, there's no lag time on its benefits and no risk of completely losing your life as you now know it.

It's amazing when you think about all of the great things that comedy can do for us. A friend once confided, "I stopped eating red meat 'cause it's got too much blood pressure." The good news is, that person's not your doctor. The even better news is that comedy actually reduces your blood

26

pressure! Here's the skinny. (Do you like the way I threw in that word *skinny* when we're talking about health benefits. No really. That's just a bonus. I'm not even going to charge more for that.) According to the American College of Sports Medicine, watching comedy improves your blood flow. This is not surprising if you think about it. While you're watching a show, you're relaxed, you're easygoing, and your body is vibrating with laughter. Compare that to a horror movie where you're frozen with fear, or a documentary that makes you completely irritated at yourself for having eaten something other than lettuce. This, not surprisingly, constricts blood flow by about 18 percent. So, the next time you see someone having a heart attack, remember your CPR training—thirty chest compressions, open the airway, tilt the patient's head toward the screen, queue Eddie Murphy's *Delirious*, and press play.

In addition to improving blood flow, comedy also stimulates your mind. We know this not because *you think* you feel more stimulated. Oh no. I mean, c'mon. We can't trust the likes of *you*. After all, *you* enjoy comedy! What credibility do *you* have?! *We*, ahem, read it in a book. That's right. *We* get our facts where they can be trusted—from "boring people." People like Alice Isen, from the University of Maryland, (by the way, Alice, I really don't think you're boring; that was just to keep people stimulated. Okay bye.) Anyway, Alice put people into separate groups and had them watch different types of media. One group of people won the proverbial study lottery and got to watch comedy. The rest of the participants watched, well, something else. After viewing, the research team quizzed the participants with simple associative questions. And what they found was significant. The group that didn't watch comedy answered 25 percent fewer answers than those who watched it. Apparently, they just replied with a "No, I'm not stimulated enough to answer that right now." Where was that brilliant line when I was in college?! And here I thought alcohol and drugs killed brain cells. The real culprit is "boring people."

Comediology

Clearly comedy is a great thing for our wellness and mental health. But we often only seek and embrace it when we leave the office. Apparently, there is no place for comedy at our job; we're too busy working on being efficient and cost-effective. This, by the way, is *exactly* why I drink water *on the way* to the bathroom. It totally saves me a trip later. Do you know how much this is adding to the bottom line, people? Seriously genius!

If you want to hate your life, burn out on your career, and die with your face buried in Excel, but, you know, this time *without* all of the glory, then this is clearly the path for you. As an added bonus, it comes in two flavors. You can die young and under the grand delusion that you were well liked and respected by all. "Wait, you were the guy that did all those Excel formulas right? Yeeaah, I remember you. You were awesome. Totally. Ummm . . . can I just slide around you so I can get another butter cream? Or, alternatively, you can kick the bucket as an old curmudgeon with really bad "morning breath" that smells of Metamucil and Sizzler. The choice is yours.

We've got this great thing in comedy that has been scientifically proven to help us. It helps us overcome difficult situations by "calling it like it is." By doing this, health benefits sprinkle across the land like your pet rabbit's fecal pebbles. So, why not use it?

There are big, fat elephants in just about every corporate room I've been in, but, in many cases, they are too awkward, weird, or contentious to be put on the table directly. Comedy helps get them to a place where we can discuss them in a very real way. But *you* have to open the door. You have to start by shifting these topics into a comedic light. How can you make the topic approachable by making it funny and nonthreatening? How can you diminish the veil between the analytical and the emotional? How can you tap into the "fun" and "funny" of the other people working with you? They've got it inside of them, just like you do. You just have to trust that it's there and engage it. I truly believe that every one of us has that joy within us.

However, a weird thing happens to us every Sunday night when we hear the "tick . . . tick . . . tick" of *60 Minutes* and realize that we have to work the next day. Our sphincter shrivels to the size of Willy Nelson's retirement account and we ditch everything that is extraneous to serving "the man." This includes laughing, humor and levity. But *we* have the power to bring it back.

Just like anything, it takes practice to make the shift, but once you do it, it opens the door. To improve something, you have to accept the way

Comediology

it is, *right now*. Not how you want it to be. Not how you hope it will be. Not how it looks after combing it over and applying obscene amounts of pomade and some "touch up" saliva, but just like it is now. Comedy helps us call that spade a spade and, because it's funny, bring it into a place of emotion rather than judgment. This helps us get to acceptance in a non-defensive manner. Once we're there, we are no longer burdened with disillusion. We no longer expend energy on paranoia and denial. We are open and free to exchange ideas and improve situations.

When you feel caught between "this direction is asinine" and "I don't feel like I have a choice," congratulations! This is the perfect place to use comedy. And don't worry about silly stuff like "risking it all." You're already doing this by living in the land of make-believe thinking that somehow, "everyone else" will see the truth and solve it. The fact is, "everyone else" is too worried about something called "everyone else." Make a choice to be different and wake up the masses. Do it with comedy.

A great example of using comedy comes from Adam Grant's Book, *Originals*. In his book, he references entrepreneur, Rufus Griscom. Rufus had founded a startup and was in the process of pitching it to potential investors. Now think about this scenario for a moment and put yourself in Rufus's shoes. You are the owner of a startup. You are convinced of its future success and, in turn, you've convinced a small army to join you— your two friends and their two friends and those two friends' two friends. And, yes, amazingly, you all use the same shampoo. To your shock, they signed up despite a salary cut and losing out on their opportunity to become French fry associate at All-American Burger.

Seemingly in an instant, you've transitioned from up-and-coming hipster entrepreneur who DJ's and does table magic to a Midwestern CEO who wears Dockers and brown shoes. Many people are now depending on you—employees for a paycheck, investors for a return, and insurance companies for exorbitant health premiums. Recently you've been trying to keep up with demands on a shoestring budget. As a result, you've been running the operation like a Vietnamese sweatshop with the promise of a brighter day, a day where employees would be released from their Chatter, Slack bots, and bio-waste tubes if only to play one game on the beloved foosball table, your strategic recruiting tool for Millennials. "You guys have a foosball table?!" "That's right, Jimmy, and you'll get to walk by it and the hepatitis-infested ball pit every day on the way to your prison-cube."

In the meantime, however, you need money. You feel like you're storming the beaches of Normandy with two dead ferrets and a broken lampshade. You're consumed with all-nighters, biting your fingernails, and living on Top Ramen, something you swore you would never do once you passed your final college course, "Entrepreneurship 101." Oh, the irony.

Now, lo and behold, you have a potential investor who is interested. *Very interested.* The pivotal step is simple: they want you to pitch the company to them. Okay, cool, this is simple and obvious, right? For your presentation, you're going to use the "Facebook Strategy." You will present vague headlines like "Winning in the New Age." You'll combine pictures of smiling employees or, if that fails, random drunk people. You'll have your workers "like" the pictures and provide in-depth commentary like "OMG" or "LMAO," lending good insight into the company's culture. Moreover, you'll talk about all three of your prospective customers and all the others you could get with just a little more money. You could also tell them how this funding is going to enable you to rule the world. And, provided basic minor assumptions hold true, like it won't be cold in Russia during wintertime, you will soon be profitable. You could talk right up to the top of the hour and then generously leave twenty seconds or so for questions.

The investors don't need to know that payroll is typically late. Nor do they need to know that your only customer is threatening to not renew, and the annual plan went completely out the window once we realized that Millennials have no idea what our flagship product, a "magazine," actually is, much less want to purchase one. You'll just tell them the good things and trust that, like other socioeconomic events of great importance such as speed dating and presidential debates, facts must be taken at face value.

This feels like a lot of corporate situations I've been in. There is so much fear in the current situation and the natural tendency is to "cover it up." After all, we all are keenly aware that if a bomb is placed in your hands and you haven't dismantled it by the time other people find out about it, you're clearly the culprit. Right? Right?! Say it. Say it!!! With this pressure, we tend to get too serious about ourselves and our situation. We delude ourselves into thinking that "calling it like it is" or "asking for help" are

Comediology

shameful acts to be embraced only by weak souls or Jimmy Stewart at Christmastime, when in fact they are true strengths. We even put more pressure on ourselves into thinking that, to resolve a situation, we need to get even more serious and stressed. We even go so far as to point fingers at other people and situations versus owning the truth.

To highlight this effect, I'd like to take a quick detour into my youth. We'll return to our hero Rufus shortly. When I was a late teen, I worked at an art supply warehouse along with all of the other presidential hopefuls. My job, along with a few other irresponsible slackers, was to pick, pack, and ship art supplies. Most of the time, these art supplies were small items like paint brushes and writing pads. Sometimes, however, the supplies were very large, like wall-size poster frames and oversized sheet glass.

One day, a couple of coworkers, Vince and Julio, were moving several expensive pieces of this enormous sheet glass up a flight of stairs. Vince, or, as Julio pronounced it, "Beence," was one of the "rising stars" of the warehouse. And Julio was a recent import from Mexico who had yet to prove himself among these highly competent, cutthroat, junior art supply warehouse laborers.

The pieces themselves were about twelve feet long and four feet wide and there were eight pieces to a load. The load itself was awkward because it was long—which, coincidentally, is something my wife once said to me after a juice cleanse. And it was heavy because, duh, it weighed a lot. Easily over two hundred pounds, it was a struggle for even three people to load, and here two were making the attempt.

Julio was at the bottom carrying the lion's share of the weight up the stairs. Vince was leading, shouldering some of the burden but mostly guiding Julio to the top of the stairs. The stairs were in plain view from the work floor, so as they ascended, we, the crew, enjoyed the entertainment of watching them struggle—ah, now, this is the life!

About halfway up the stairs, something happened. I'm not sure if Julio got tired, unfocused, or just lost his footing, but the load started to jiggle. Starting at the bottom, which was Julio's end, it wobbled back and forth as both Julio and Vince tried to get a handle on it. After a few moments, the quiver proved to be too much for Julio to control. With a panic-stricken look in his eyes, he made a decision that would forever change the fate of the thousand-dollar glass load and simultaneously Joe Bob's Insurance (no longer in business). He quickly pulled his hands away from under the glass, turned his body, and jumped down several stairs. With no support from the bottom, the large load of glass immediately came crashing down.

We all heard the loud "Cablash!" We saw thousands of pieces of glass fly in every direction. It was unnerving and the entire crew was in shock. Both Julio and Vince watched helplessly from the stairs. At this point, there was nothing anyone could do. We all just stood there in a silent stupor for about thirty seconds looking at the mess. Then we looked at each other.

After some time, all eyes fixed on Julio. The crew realized that we were all going to have to work double time to clean up this horrific mess. Everyone clearly knew who was responsible for dropping the load and, consequently, we were not happy with him. I'm sure that our glares revealed just that.

You could clearly see the chagrin on Julio's face. There was no place for him to run and nowhere to hide. He looked down. It was abundantly obvious to him and everyone else that he had dropped the ball and he was clearly embarrassed and humiliated.

After a few seconds of painfully awkward silence, Julio looked up from his daze. His eyes met each of ours as if to get our attention. Then, with one finger accusingly pointing up to the stairs, he announced with authority, "Eet was Beence."

After about a second of digesting what Julio said, a few of us started snickering. The snickers soon gave way to giggling and an instant later we were all laughing uncontrollably. It was so blatantly obvious that it was Julio's fault. The way he was trying to cover it up was simply comical.

The laughter went on for several minutes. Even Julio himself apparently concluded that his throwing Beence under the bus was funny and started laughing, too. This made it even funnier.

Although we all enjoyed the laugh, from that point forward we all slightly distrusted Julio. What if *we* were carrying a heavy load with him and something happened when people *weren't* around to witness what had actually transpired? Would we be carelessly thrown under the art supply delivery truck too? Would we get grief for damaging company goods or, worse yet, lose our jobs? We all distanced ourselves from Julio and I'm sure he felt it. No one wanted to partner with him on work matters or friendship—which, not surprisingly, are both based on trust.

Comediology

Julio lived on, sure, but he never made it to the glorious heights in Art Supply for which he had potential. I think he later moved into cheeseburger mechanics, but I lost track of him after that.

I think things would have been different if Julio had embraced some light-heartedness. Levity could have provided a moment of perspective, allowing him to realize that this is not, in fact, the end of the world. Julio could have accepted responsibility, and maybe even laughed at it from the get-go, rather than after he covered it up. From a coworker perspective, we would have much preferred this to his immediately blaming Vince. Had you been in Julio's shoes, you might have used humor or self-deprecation to let others see that you got it as well. Something like, "Oh dear God, the glass has fallen and it can't get up" or "Thank you all for coming. It's nice that you could all witness me at the pinnacle moment of my career" or "That's the sound of you all needing a new coworker" or even, "Hilary Clinton can't break a glass ceiling but apparently I can." Using comedy, which inherently forces you to acknowledge the truth, would have put Julio on a different trajectory.

Although the glass incident is a fond memory that still makes me chuckle, it demonstrates our natural and societal tendency to hide the truth when it is not "good." This propensity is so strong in us, it can overrule our basic logic. "My pants are down. My hand is bright red. It's elbow-deep in the cookie jar and the blood on the glove matches my DNA. Yeah, I can totally get away with this one—eet was Beence." I used to get angered by people who tried to talk other people into their innocence when they were clearly guilty. Do they think everyone else is that dumb?! Now, however, I realize, that it has nothing to do with the appraisal of another's intelligence; rather, something in how our brains are hardwired discourages us from divulging anything that might invite a threat.

From a survival perspective, this "protection" makes sense. Functionally speaking, however, and how it plays out in everyday life, we're clearly "cracking smoke." We make it hard on ourselves when we're backed into a corner. We curl up into a fetal ball resembling a fist with one reproachful digit pointing at "someone else," when all we really need is some levity. After all, levity enables us to take a step back. It provides us with perspective. It gives us a little relief and space to acknowledge the truth. That done, we can let ourselves be seen by others, and let it be. This will not only inherently help us but also enable others to relate and help us too.

Back to Rufus Griscom's story from *Originals*. I'm happy to say that Rufus worked through this tendency. He embraced the present moment and didn't become defensive. He called it like it was and let in some levity.

He didn't start his presentation with, "Here's what's so great about me and my company," nor did he start with, "So this is how I'm different from my competition." He didn't even start with a problem statement, which clearly strays from my fifth-grade teacher's critical writing technique— risky move, Rufus, risky.

Instead, he started with a slide titled "The Top 5 Reasons Not to Invest in My Startup." This, by the way, went over much better than, "Eeet was Beence!"

At a first glance, when you think about Rufus's approach, it's kind of like going up to a person you really like and saying, "Hi. Name's Bill. Yeah. Just don't think this thing is gonna work out." If that wasn't bad enough, he then detailed each of the five reasons. Which, to further the analogy, is like saying. "See that mole right there. Yeah? Well, if you look closely, you'll see it's got a nasty hair growing out of it. Oh yeah, and I fart a lot, too."

The approach was most unexpected and the effect was captivating to say the least. Being the founder, traditionally Rufus would naturally default to being the "salesperson" in this scenario. His responsibility is to sell the company as an investment, highlighting all positive aspects while minimizing the negative ones.

The investor, on the other hand, is an "evaluator" of the proposal. They are there to ask questions to get past the salesperson's smokescreen because, after all, some salespeople will sell you gravity and promise that it will take you to the moon and stars and goes great as a creamy spread on a Ritz cracker.

This meeting between the founder and investors is like a first date. Yes, they've read the bio, but "I love music and nature" doesn't give you a lot to go on. Now it's time to determine if the other person is in any way a freak show without any corresponding niceties like a strong desire for intimacy, the ability to cook a succulent blackened salmon, or a strong desire for intimacy. Sorry, my bad. I thought eight minutes had passed.

Comediology

But Rufus turned the tables. He didn't tell them he loved music and hiking. He told them how he crapped in his bed just last Saturday. Figuratively, anyway. The investors weren't expecting his honest, forthright, and, well, comedic launch. "Wait a minute, did he just tell me that he's a moody mama's boy who only washes his toes when he's in the community hot tub? Well, now that I know the truth, what the hell am I supposed to do here for the next three hours? What's my value add? And where's the damned blackened salmon?!"

While this approach is seemingly a train wreck, Rufus accomplished three key things that enabled his success: he made them laugh, he earned their trust, and he transformed the outcome.

Rufus Made Them Laugh

Rufus started the meeting with a surprise, a tool frequently used in comedy. As a result, he made the investors laugh. This helped him bypass their analytical and skeptical cerebral cortex and plug in to the creamy Oreo part of their brain, the limbic system, which creates emotional connections. Rufus and the company he founded were obviously impressive to them; otherwise, they wouldn't be there. As is often the case, he didn't need to go out of his way to *prove* anything. In fact, *trying* to prove it could have worked against him. Why? Because, at the end of the day, we're all human beings. Connection is fulfilling and meaningful and important to all of us. They weren't there to meet a calculator—"Here's the number four, now let's see how you carry it." They were there to build a *relationship*, and in so doing, vet Rufus as a person.

Relationships, as we all know, are built over time. They require openness and vulnerability to establish the emotional connection. Comedy helps facilitate this. Conversely, it's very difficult to *prove* a relationship. This is *exactly* why I stopped carrying my abacus on dates. Don't you wish ya boyfriend knew math like me? Don't ya?

The investors knew Rufus's professional credentials, but they didn't know *him*. Was he narcissistic and psychotic? Or was he self-aware, humane, and human? His opening slide told them that he saw the truth despite running an intense and cash-drained startup. This, we know, is like drinking optimism through a razor-thin straw of self-denial or joining the Tea Party. He was a guy who could call it like it is, or he had

35

found the ideal concoction of prescription medication. Either way, it was a thumbs-up.

Rufus Earned Their Trust

The second thing Rufus did with his approach is that he was real. In comedy, if you muddle reality, people get bored fast. To keep their attention, you must earn their trust, and you do this by speaking the truth. You must be true about the situation, your emotions, and your outlook.

Take, for example, my six-year-old, Charlie. He was wrangling my wedding ring from my finger, claiming, "I want to be married to mommy."

I asked, "Well, wouldn't you rather be married to someone your own age?"

He shook his head angrily and said, "No. Mommy."

"Well, how about a friend's mommy?"

He stood strong, saying again, "No. Mommy."

"Hmmm" I inquired, "how about someone you love like Mommy, say, Grandma?"

His face contorted in a surprised and horrified expression as he angrily retorted, "Grandma's almost dead. I want mommy!"

This, by the way, is why I believe children are such great comedians. It's not because they were born with the ability to write amazing jokes, but simply because they're honest about situations. Well, honest in their minds anyway—Grandma is alive, well, and thankfully not "almost dead."

In comedy, you need to hold the audience's attention to the punch line. The same is true in business. In both cases, for this to happen, they need to be able to identify with your context and your story. It must be true for them, or at least *credible* as it pertains to their thoughts, feelings, and experiences.

Rufus knew that if he conveyed only the good things, he would lose believability because, let's face it, who takes a challenging journey like this one and finds nothing but rose petals and chocolate-covered zebra balls (too much on the zebra balls?). Moreover, unchecked optimism is just plain annoying. If Rufus had used this approach, he would no longer be a reliable source of credible and complete information for his investors. In this way, Rufus's approach was brilliant. By being *real*, he saved everyone

Comediology

a lot of time, enhanced his credibility, and created a bond of trust. He also created another kind of bond. A James "Bond."

Taking a step back, we realize that, to be real, Rufus had to first be real with himself. Well, duh—this seems abundantly obvious. However, when you think about it, how many times have we disillusioned ourselves by either not recognizing, not realizing, or not accepting the truth? Never, you say? Right. Okay, then, how many times has a "friend" disillusioned him or herself?

It's funny how you can be blind to your own denial, but can see a friend's denial like the splotches on a painter's overalls. By the way, isn't there a better color for these guys than "white"? Most of the time, there's not a lot you can do to help others see the truth. You tell them your opinion repeatedly. You tell them other's opinions. You provide examples. You show them photographs, fingerprints, recordings, and black gloves with DNA. But to no avail. "He didn't mean to gamble away our life savings; he just got bad tips from many thoroughbred race horses and of course we believed him because he told us that they came straight from the horse's mouth. "That's the way it is and they're going to believe it until, well, they don't. It's so frustrating when the truth is in plain sight but they just can't see it. So when someone comes along who *does* see truth, especially about themselves, it's refreshing. You subconsciously have respect for this person because they don't placate themselves with fantasies, but live in truth no matter how stressful or distasteful. You admire them further because, to get to this place of acceptance, they not only had to listen to themselves, but also trust their truth and share it confidently with others.

Finally, we understand that to improve anything, we first need to see it for what it is, and you can't do that by living on Fantasy Island. We've got mad respect for Rufus because he listens to himself, he trusts it. Moreover, we want to partner with him because he doesn't hide behind a shiny façade of manufactured "perfection." He's "real" and this directly connects with our own "real."

Rufus Transformed the Outcome

We've all been in "judge and jury" meetings. These gatherings essentially come down to "finding the witch" and "burning him or her," not necessarily in that order. I believe that these meetings often result

Chris S. Tabish with Kurtis Matthews

this way because one, tensions are high (it's corporate America), and two, meeting attendees either can't relate to the presenter or don't understand their context for action or decision.

Rufus changed this. He transformed a potential Salem witch trial to a twenty-first-century meeting using collaboration and brainstorming.

With his unorthodox approach, Rufus got the investors to identify with the main characters of the story—him and his company—as well as understand the contextual setting of the characters. They had witnessed enough "humanity" from Rufus to feel like they could relate. They also understood the trials and tribulations from his point of view. Rufus's transformational plot was not unlike a three-part story, a common structure used in screenwriting that divides narrative into three parts. The first, typically called the *setup*, introduces the main character. The second, the *confrontation*, outlines the issues they are facing. The third and final part, the *resolution*, describes the conclusion of the character as it pertains to their confrontation and is usually accompanied by inspirational music with visual depictions of a UFO, caped man, or overly verbose rodent triumphantly soaring beyond the Earth's stratosphere.

If the setup or confrontation is not portrayed well, we either don't understand the situation, don't agree with the main character's point of view, or we simply don't give a shiznickel. Some movies portray this brilliantly. Others are titled *Batman v. Superman*. The movies that do employ this effectively parse the information out very strategically. We sometimes end up furious at the main character for decisions they made or actions they took. Then, when we're given more complete information, we are in awestruck admiration of them. We change our opinion because *now* we see their humanity, relate to their point of view, and understand their motives.

This works the same way in comedy and in corporate America. If the audience thinks you're mean, bitter, arrogant, or just pathetic, they aren't going to relate to your setup and your punch line will be lost. If you can get the audience aligned to the main character—you—they will see and experience things from your point of view. But up to that point, they are evaluating you. They haven't yet taken you in. The good news is that once they do, they will bestow gifts upon you such as the "benefit of the doubt,"

Comediology

"selfless desire for you to succeed" and sandwiches, lots of sandwiches. What is it with these people and sandwiches?!

All this because you put yourself on the table before them with authenticity. You connected with them and you were vulnerable and open about your issues. How can you do any better than that? We all know life isn't perfect, so the best thing we can hope for is to receive genuine and open communication. This is what Rufus did. Once this mind meld is done, the audience and the presenter merge, collectively resolving the problems that jointly lay before them. They could see things the way Rufus did and understand the decisions he made. Even if they couldn't, they would give him the benefit of the doubt because he's open, honest, funny, and likeable.

The following is what the transformation might have looked like as it pertained to Rufus's presentation:

Before the Transformation:

Rufus: Did I come off as arrogant or insincere when I talked about how world domination was in our grasp and these *were* the droids they were looking for?

Investment Group: I'm not sure I'm buying his story. He just doesn't have enough leadership experience and, well, "Johnny Blaze" to understand the real issues associated with world domination. And he certainly doesn't have the prerequisite facial hair.

After the Transformation:

All: That meeting was awesome! I really feel like we're working together as a team. Now, if we could just give Rufus a couple of weeks of Jedi training and roller-tape away all that damned Wookiee hair, I think we could have a go.

I think of how many times I've had a meeting under the first scenario. I used to think it had to do with the content. Now, however, the first thing I look to is my *humanity*. Moreover, I often do this through the lens of comedy. Why comedy? Because one is not possible without the other. To employ comedy means that you are being real, sincere, authentic, truthful, flawed, vulnerable, and, well, human.

The transformation in the second scenario aligned everyone to work on the same problem with the same underlying goal and point of view. From experience, I know that this significantly reduces tension levels and increases fulfillment. I imagine everyone left that meeting feeling like a key player, collectively chartered with conquering the mountain as a team versus trying to outdo their opponent.

Oh, yeah, you were probably curious as to Rufus's result. Despite telling the investors his top five reasons not to buy his company, they bought it anyway. Moreover, he did the same thing two years later when he sold a second company, Babble, to the Disney Corporation. Simply put, as Borat would say, "He is great success, U, S, AND A. Very excite!" All of this because he kept it real with a little comedy.

This is but one example of many. Want a few others? Just watch any form of advertising and you'll see the powerful tool of comedy eroding the analytical and connecting with the emotional. No one notices this stealthy ally because they're too busy laughing. But, like Tom Cruise breaking into a secret defense facility in *Mission Impossible*, that comedy is hard at work sneakily connecting with the emotion of your audience. Dun-dun dundun dun-dun. Dundun dun-dun. Dundun dun-dun. Dun-dun—da-da-daaaa. Yes that was the theme song from *Mission Impossible*—sheesh, people! Then, before you know it, the seed is planted. You think of the content because it brings you joy. You share it with friends because it's funny. Where you resisted previously, you no longer oppose. Where previously you were not open, you now consider. In time, you may even conform. What do you have when you hold two green balls in your hand? Yes, Kermit the Frog's undivided attention. And it's no different here. Comedy has you in its grasp and it's useless to resist it. You're a baadd comedy, baaaad!

You know those commercials that showcase the latest and greatest pharmaceutical drug that promises to alleviate some unwanted symptom with the small price to pay of potential side effects such as halitosis, anal leakage, or everlasting shame? Can you recall just one of them by name? No? Hmmm. . . . Conversely, if I were to say to you, "It is not often that I have unforeseen halitosis and anal leakage, but when I do it is because I drink . . . " Okay maybe not word for word, Mr. Auditor! But I bet you still got it, right? Dos Equis, of course—that's easy.

Comediology

Why can't we remember the other pharmaceutical drug names? Well, for starters, why would we want to? After all, the drugs themselves sound dangerous. They seem to have side effects WAY worse than what they're being used to alleviate. Next, the commercials are always the same—an older man playing fetch with his dog, a woman being depressed, or an elderly couple about to fornicate . . . eeewwwww. I already get all this every time Uncle Ernie and Aunt Mildred come to visit. Why do I need a commercial?

Finally, the disclaimers are ridiculous. Do these companies realize how bad they sound? The message is like one of those horrific deals you get from a *Twilight Zone* genie—"Yes, I'll ease your nonstop yoga flatulence and give you the girl of your dreams, but you'll no longer have dental coverage and skin. Mwah ha ha! Ahem, uh sorry about that. Deal?" Their marketing departments must be run by copyright attorneys, Montgomery Burns, and, oh, I don't know . . . SATAN?!

And you see, there it is. The messaging never got past my analytical brain. I'm still evaluating it and the result is not favorable. Hint: The result is *never* favorable when you are "still evaluating it." It's like being stuck in the friend zone without the help of breath mints, alcohol, or a Members Only jacket.

Conversely, let's look at our beloved Dos Equis beer commercial. Wait a minute? That's alcohol! And alcohol is bad for you! Its unplanned and harmful side effects include traffic accidents, liver damage, and two-thirds of the people from Salt Lake City, Utah (I would know, I'm one of them!). But wait, it's Dos Equis! The most interesting man in the world endorses Dos Equis. He's funny, man—we love that guy! Well, the original one anyway. He gives us brilliantly funny lines like, "He lives vicariously through himself" or "He once won a staring contest with his own reflection" or "He once won the World Series of Poker using UNO cards." Sure, alcohol can be bad, but this isn't just alcohol, this is Dos Equis!

And there it is, the magic of comedy hard at work justifying our sins. You bought in and didn't even realize you were doing it. It's unconscious and automatic.

While the advertising industry is obviously utilizing comedy very effectively, no other industry has fully explored its potential, with one

Chris S. Tabish with Kurtis Matthews

notable exception—traffic school. What? Really, all other industries? Of all things, you're going to let "traffic school" surpass you in *any* category, much less this one?! These are government-sponsored agencies, people, yet they're effectively using comedy better than most corporations out there. Let me say it another way: comedy traffic school is a grape-juice-stained stuffed Chihuahua wallowing in Uncle Ron's sweat ring, and it's winning Best in Show!

Aside from all the scientific and business benefits you will receive through leveraging comedy, there is one other critical reason for using it. Simply put, it's FUN! Yes, that's right—*FUN!* Don't forget fun in your life. It's like your dad walking in front of the television naked—just *don't*. Haven't you noticed what happens when you forget fun in your life? You get grumpy, irritable, and impatient. And not surprisingly, *this* is when you meet all the assholes. They never come out when you're happy and enjoying your life, so it's apparently a universal law. Look it up. It's under "N" for "Naked Dad/Not Using Comedy."

You must bring levity to your work life. If you "tolerate" your work, you'll definitely need it, but it's essential even if you love what you do. When we are having fun, we do our best and we enjoy ourselves. Doing our best creates momentum to persevere and do great things. So, use comedy more in your life. Have fun and watch in amazement as the awesomeness unveils.

Comediology

Summary

Yes, it's time for the recap. Don't worry, you won't need bonding glue for that dynamite hairpiece. Here goes . . .

1) **Accept the way things are right now**. Realize that to figure out the solution, you must first accept that there is a problem. And also remember, "Denial" ain't just a river in Africa.

2) **Embrace comedy**. Add levity to connect with others and open yourself up to more possibilities. A simple way to do this is to ask yourself, "What's funny about this situation?"

3) **Align your audience to your point of view**. Be real with the situation and own it. This will earn you credibility and enable you to explore solutions together and is much more preferred than "Eet was Beence." Align the audience to your point of view with emotion and trust that your authentic emotion will connect to theirs.

4) **Ask for help**. Don't deny people the gift to help. People *love* to help and will jump at the chance provided 1) they can and 2) they resonate with your point of view and situation.

5) **Have fun**. And, if you're a dad, don't walk in front of the TV naked.

Honesty is the key to a relationship. If you can fake that, you're in.

—*Richard Jeni*

You've Got to Feel It to Make Them Believe It

I love it when my six-year-old son Charlie tells a joke. Having said that, it typically comes in three flavors. Flavor one: I've heard the joke before, probably from a refined comedic venue like the back of a Lucky Charms Box. Flavor two: It's not even a joke, but a riddle, question, or observation with seemingly no punch line. Flavor three: I haven't a clue what he's talking about.

Regardless of the flavor, here's the beautiful part—I find myself laughing, often hysterically, at all his "jokes." Why is that?

It's simple. I laugh because he laughs. But why does *he* laugh? He laughs because he thinks what he is saying is the funniest thing *ever*. In doing so, he *feels* the funny of what he is saying. He's not just saying the words; he's completely absorbed in the joke. *He feels it in the fiber of his being.* And let me tell you, that kid eats *lots* of fiber—shooo. Consequently, the funny bubbles up inside of him. He is completely and utterly entertained by his own "joke" and, as the recipient, I find it absolutely mesmerizing and hilarious. In fact, most times, he struggles to get the words out because he's so consumed with laughing at his own joke.

To Charlie, it doesn't matter what I do at that point. I could laugh with him, which, of course, makes him laugh more. Alternatively, I could hold a straight face, which, of course, entices him to laugh more. In many ways, my actions are irrelevant to his joy. He's enjoying the moment so thoroughly because he has felt the funniness of this thought, and while he shares it, he's feeling the same funny. This is such an amazing and beautiful moment between us; it is one of my favorites with my son.

At this point, it doesn't matter who is the "giver" of the joke and who is the "receiver." We are sharing a moment of pure funny through laughter, and we are both active participants. We might share the same funny thought, or we might not, but we definitely share the same *feeling* of funny. It's kind of like the common cold. It doesn't matter how you got it—you're going to sneeze green boogers just like ugly people.

Behind every comedy act, there a lot of steps. First, you generate the material and create the funny. Then you memorize the material while rehearsing your act. We get feedback on the joke and tweak it here and there. This is an iterative process that easily lends itself to our getting bored with the joke or too caught up in the mechanics of delivery: the right words, the right inflection, the right body movement, the right emphasis on the phrase "your mama," and so on. And, if we're not careful, we can LOSE the most important thing in delivering the joke, the *magic* that connects everyone—the funny. Or more specifically, we lose our *feeling* of why we find the joke funny.

We laugh when a child is telling a joke because *they* find it funny. Likewise, and although not as obvious, you can tell when a comedian genuinely *feels* their material. They *feel* the frustration, the confusion, the ridiculousness of it all—*they feel the things that make it funny. This* is a key ingredient in making it entertaining and funny for everyone else.

It's true. The mechanics of memorizing your act are not unlike rehearsing a performance, a ballet, a football play, or a speech. Knowing your material is essential. But this is only the surface. We didn't come here for the mechanics. We came for the human spirit. I hear it's to die for.

There's a quote by Roger Ebert that says, "It's not what a movie is about, it's *how* it is about it." And just like stand-up or life, it's not about the "what" but about the "how" that makes it interesting. Know the "why" and feel the "how." Because *knowing* the "why" gives you the direction, and *feeling* the "how" is the magic that gets you there. Moreover, it's what makes the comedian bulletproof before an audience. If you're focused on the audience reaction, you might as well be waiting for an axe to fall. You've got to focus on what you can control and are certain to enjoy—*you've got to feel your funny.* This is what gives a comedian the audacity to feel things in front of many people and not give a hoot as to what the audience thinks of them. Yes, even when they're not on Valium. They aren't acting up there. They aren't trying to be what you think they should be. They are going to feel what they feel because they feel it. So what if you don't find it funny? *It doesn't matter.*

Comediology

You convey *thoughts* through your *words*. However, you convey *feelings* through *everything else*—your eyes, your voice, your posture, your hand movement, and yes, even that grind thing you do at the club that is so completely gross, yet simultaneously, so "delish"—yowza! Sometimes your spoken material is, in fact, strong enough to stand on its own. This is called "reading." Other than that, your *feelings* are what resonates with the audience. Albert Mehrabian, Professor Emeritus of Psychology at UCLA, has produced well-known publications on this very topic. He claims that words convey only 7 percent of our meaning. Vocal expression conveys 38 percent. And our body language conveys a whopping 55 percent. In other words, 93 percent of what the audience will remember and believe comes down to what you convey non-verbally from your feelings, nothing more than feelings.

We all have different thoughts and biases. We have different political preferences, views about the economy, and personal aspirations. This all wires us to *think* very differently from one another. However, in its most pure and simple form, *we all experience the same feelings*: joy, humor, surprise, and so forth. After all, at its core, is your feeling of joy any different from my feeling of joy? What?! You think yer joy is better 'n mine?! It may come from a different thought, and probably does, but the core feeling is the same.

What I learned from stand-up comedy is that thoughts may or may not translate, but *feelings are universal and contagious*. Just watch Robin Williams for five minutes. First off, what in the world was he talking about? And, if anyone else read the script, provided there was one, would it be funny? Maybe. But I guarantee not all of it, and certainly not in the full way that he delivers it. That guy was the embodiment of feeling his funny on stage, and it was a blast to participate and watch the funny unravel from within him.

This is exactly why music can influence our mood. Music is not just data, and you can't factually prove why a certain song is uplifting, sad, or simply, "bringin' sexy back". Music has existed in all societies throughout documented history, the only exception being Utah, where the movie *Footloose* was filmed. With music, the creator expresses the "feeling" and we experience the same "feeling." Stand-up comedy, while seemingly less apparent, is, in fact, no different.

47

Chris S. Tabish with Kurtis Matthews

Comediology

Fairfield, California. I was in the audience listening to a client presentation. It was a large meeting. There were at least a hundred people in the room and fifty on the phone bridge. This meeting was critical, as the company client was providing key information that would help numerous companies, including mine, bid for a large opportunity. In other words, we were trying to win some business.

The host for the meeting was a woman named Sandy. She was the corporate representative that would be "front and center" on stage kicking things off. Sandy could best be described as the epitome of corporate America. Well, just the annoying part anyway. She had a Church Lady demeanor with a North Dakota accent akin to Tina Fey playing Sarah Palin. With her presentation style, you felt like a second grader with teacher at the board. Is Sandy too going to crush *all* of our dreams? It was clear that she believed the concepts she presented were slightly, or completely, beyond your comprehension. She spoke impatiently with condescension. It was as if the frustration of continually being asked to clarify was implicit in her tone of voice. So, she was efficient. I'll give her that.

She opened the meeting with an, "Ohhh keah everybody, I'm gonna need you to pay attention here, yeah? This is really important stuff here and we've just got a little bit of time so you really need to pay attention here, mmmkkkay?" She laid out the agenda and then started in with content, "Ohhh kay, as you can see, this policy, kay, is going into effect immediately, kay, which means it's gonna start real soon here. For those with any questions on the policy, kay, you can go to—." She was cut off mid-sentence.

From the back of the room, which was about fifty rows from the stage, the double doors swung wide open. In fact, they were so forcefully thrown ajar that they loudly bounced against the connecting walls. Tony, the company's Chief Technology Officer, apparently doing his best John Wayne "new guy in town" act, strutted in a few paces and then halted. Swaggering in unannounced, he entered with such a ruckus, people couldn't help themselves from turning to see what the commotion was about. Sure, it was smack dab in the middle of Sandy's presentation, but that was no concern of Tony's.

Comediology

Apropos of nothing, he started loudly spewing what to him was most likely sound advice to the masses. However, we were in a large auditorium and he wasn't holding a microphone. So, while everyone could see Tony, his speech came across as loud mumbles making him sound like a mentally unstable radish farmer or Jabba the Hutt. . "Doggy dah rara doomsdayer Solo chan Wookiee!" Uhhh . . . what in the hell did he just say?! I turned to the person next to me, who shrugged his shoulders as if to infer, "Sorry, I never got around to Episode VI."

Suffice to say, no one had a clue what Tony was saying. A few moments later and evidently finished, he stood erect and visibly proud of his apparent achievement in speech. His body language seemed to say, "I'm now available for handshakes and autographs." Seeing he was done with whatever he felt like he said, we all turned around in our chairs to return to Sandy and the soul degradation at hand.

Confusion rapidly turned to frustration as Sandy's slightly condescending presentation turned into a full-fledged lecture that left us completely bewildered. "You know what?" she claimed. "That was a *really* good point that Tony was making. I hope you were all paying attention. You should all write down what Tony just said. Oh, how true, Tony, and I couldn't have said it better myself. You need to take note of this, people. Really. Mmmkay?"

From where she was standing and what she must have heard, how exactly was "RA RA DU DU" a *really* good point? Moreover, how could we have possibly written whatever language that was down? None of us in the live audience completely heard or understood the gibberish that came out of Tony's mouth, and I sure wasn't versed in radish farmer or alien-slug script. Worse, the conference phone speaker and microphone were next to Sandy, so there's no way that people on the phone could have heard it either. It was really concerning because any information being conveyed here could be the difference between winning and losing a multimillion-dollar contract.

It was abundantly obvious that Tony was the big man on campus and everyone ultimately reported to him, including Sandy. After she was finished with the final coat of Turtle Wax on his ego, there came a question on the call. "Yeah, I'm not sure what Tony said, can you please repeat it?"

49

Chris S. Tabish with Kurtis Matthews

There was a pause and Sandy looked up as if subconsciously checking if she had just soiled her pants. After a moment, she looked around the room in a panic. I don't know what she was looking for—a recording device, a fire alarm, or the "jobs" section of the local newspaper, but whatever it was, she didn't find it. She turned her body to partially face the phone as if to say, "I'll answer this question, kay, but you people really need to pay better attention, kay."

She then wrinkled her nose and giggled with a loud "hhhmmm—ha!" which made this awkward situation, well, even more awkward. She then pointed her finger while she yelled out at the top of her lungs, "It was Beence!" No not really. In reality, she answered the question with a question: "You know what?" Then she said. "I'm not really sure what he said either, mmkay. Tony, could you please repeat what you were saying?"

This woman had the bravado of a drunken Chihuahua with no idea what she was talking about! She had completely sold it as one of the greatest ideas known to modern man, but actually had no clue. It was one of the funniest things I had witnessed, but it was too embarrassing and career limiting to laugh at out loud. Going to our *Jeopardy!* Daily Double, and the answer is—"What was the key phrase that got Sandy fired last Tuesday?"

This is a clear example of faking understanding, connection, and emotion. And okay, sure, we've all done it with Aunt Marie's Christmas fruitcake, but this should be the exception. If we truly stay connected to what we are understanding, feeling, and communicating, we are being authentic. People can sense this and they trust and respect it. Anything less is just second-grade shenanigans.

Public Speaking

There are numerous public speaking courses. If you go to them like I have, you'll realize two things. First, they make you watch yourself on camera. There's no way to hide the truth—this is a very painful experience and also kills any potential dreams of appearing in adult films. While watching, I couldn't help but wonder: I actually go out in public looking this bad and my friends never told me? Seriously, people, and you call yourself my friends?! You know who you are.

Second, they'll often instruct you on how to "perform" your speech. They coach you on where to stand, what to do with your hands, and how

Comediology

to project your voice. All this so you can accomplish the presumed goal of sounding exactly like an overpriced speech coach. Wait, what? Don't get me wrong, much of this is very useful. However, these are all ultimately *tactics* of communication.

Tactics, in and of themselves, are not a bad thing. However, I believe that the best way to approach speaking in public is with a *strategy* and preferably some warm Krispy Kremes. And from my experience, the strategy is simple: have content that you believe in and allow yourself to *feel* it. If you do this, you will naturally take care of the rest. After all, when was the last time you expressed anger at someone while dancing the Charleston? (Yes, that was a quick shout-out to all my readers who were alive in the 1920s—hey y'all!). When was the last time you felt overflowing joy while curled into the fetal position, devouring a tub of Ben & Jerry's and repeating, "Oh, I'll get that crazy son' bitch, you just wait and see." My guess would be never, because, quite simply, you *feel* and *exhibit* what you *believe.*

Your physical body tells no lies. Just ask any sixth-grade boy who, while fantasizing about his dream girl, was asked to do a math problem in front of the classroom. At least I think it was math. Anyway, it's difficult, if not impossible, to conceal the way you feel. What's more, you now have a handy pointer to display your work. So . . . why hide it? Life is so much easier and less complicated when we go with the flow of our nature. And even easier still if not simultaneously asked to do math while "flowing." Oh, and believe it or not, unless you're completely cut off from any kind of feeling or self-awareness, you don't need instructions to do this. Yes, you can buy a manual. But the question is, do you really need one? Let me save you hundreds of dollars. Here goes: "Engage with your audience through eye contact," "Use inflection in your voice," and "Don't put anything in your mouth made by the Dubble Bubble company or given to you by my son." Being in alignment with your authentic message isn't difficult; it just happens if you *allow* it and don't resist it. What *is* difficult is trying to move and *act* in the way you *think* others expect. This is when we need those public speaking body-movement tips. So, I say, why not just save your hard-earned money, feel the emotions, trust in them, and let the rest take care of itself. Oh yeah, one more thing: don't daydream in math class.

Chris S. Tabish with Kurtis Matthews

Feeling your presentation doesn't start at presentation time but in the *preparation*. Why are you including this and not that? Okay, yes, check it logically, but, more importantly, how does it *feel* to you? Does it *feel* like the *right* thing to do? Are you excited? Frustrated? Certain? Uncertain? *Feel how that feels*—feel it in your body and connect to it deeply. Then, when you rehearse and ultimately present, yes, convey the information, but get in touch with the *feeling* and let your presentation come from that source.

Authenticity

Have you ever found yourself telling people what you think they want to hear? I have definitely been guilty of "sugarcoating." I've also had people tell me what they think *I* want to hear. My fourth-grade girlfriend Melissa Torgeson did this to me. By the way, Melissa, just so I'm clear, are we still taking a "small break" from our relationship, you know, just to "really appreciate" what we have together?

Truth be told, whether you're receiving or giving the sugarcoating, neither is the place to be. For whatever reason, you don't feel authenticity. You might be thinking about consequences of saying the wrong thing, hurt feelings, drama, or simply, "I just can't deal with you right now." As a result, you end up masking your emotions and blowing smoke up the butt of a pig with lipstick on it. Or something like that. Anyway. . . . The words tend to be hasty and the communication varies from relatively robotic to "sugary salesy" and carries the insincere aroma of a used car salesman who calls all his customers "Sport.". The interaction is very unfulfilling. There's no real connection and neither party makes any progress. The primary motive you are most in touch with is getting out of the present moment unscathed and running away from anything real. After all, what if the wrong thing is said?

Here's the thing, though. What makes stand-up comedians kick butt on stage is that they don't run away from their emotions. They *feel* them and they *communicate what they are feeling*. If they are afraid, they'll say it. If they are confused, in doubt, or otherwise completely lost, they'll say it. This is where their power comes from. If they were to get up there and try to placate the crowd, saying what they think people wanted to hear, they would lose the audience *quickly*. Trust me, I had to learn this the hard

Comediology

way. It's only through the communication of genuine feelings, no matter how seemingly scary, that true connection is possible.

It's the same thing with business. Have you ever observed someone at work speak from the heart and tell you that they are confused or lost or any of the other gazillion words we have for "afraid"? When that happens, I not only feel connected to them, but also gain a lot of respect for them. It's because *I trust what they are saying*. I've felt it. You can tell the difference between a smoke screen and authenticity. Like stand-up, authenticity connects you with your audience and helps you break through the matter of whatever it is you need to get through. Without it, you just kick that can down the road.

In these moments, I truly believe it's imperative to take a step back. Take a deep breath or two and connect with your true feelings. Then, when you're ready, communicate them. Just like telling a new joke for the first time on a comedy stage, you let the chips fall where they may. Not everyone will laugh at the funny. In fact, sometimes no one will. Maybe it wasn't your best night, or it was a somber crowd or a touchy subject at that time. Even when it's authentic, it still doesn't guarantee that people will resonate with your message *all* the time.

However, you've given folks the most authentic side of you. Even if they don't understand or agree, they will gain respect for you and you'll gain respect for yourself. Moreover, you won't be living in illusion, sugarcoating what you truly feel.

When you're being real, one of two things will ultimately happen. Either you will be understood and accepted and it will be perfect. Or you won't be understood or accepted, but you'll know the truth and can move forward accordingly. Therefore, it will also be perfect. But if you sugarcoat, you've got to keep living this lie. It's like walking around in Grampa Leroy's underwear—something just doesn't feel quite right, it smells funny and Grandma keeps asking you for a little "honey".

If you're in touch with your feelings and are authentically communicating them, there's nothing to fear. It either immediately confirms you are on the right path, or, alternatively, signals that this path is not in alignment with how you feel. Either way, by voicing your authenticity, you've illuminated the situation and have created an opportunity for a decision to continue or to adjust with eyes wide open. Because, think about it, would you want

Chris S. Tabish with Kurtis Matthews

to be on a journey with people who fundamentally don't understand or agree with you and how you feel? Would you want to pretend every day to be something that you're not?

Getting in touch with your true feelings and communicating them will take practice. It's simple to understand but never easy to do, at least not at first. Just like getting on that initial comedy stage, it takes courage and then practice.

To understand this better in a business context, let's go back to one of the classics. In 2004, I was managing a team; part of our jobs involved solving challenging problems for our customers using various business applications and tools available to us. My job was to work with my team and the customer to solve their problems and implement solutions.

My real challenge wasn't the work; it was my boss. While I respected and got along with her, she would either find out about these customer requests before I did or intercept them as they were in progress. Then, she would go directly to my team and start working on the solution. Or she would barge into one of our sessions and start leading the team to a solution. Every time she did this, I felt demoralized and disempowered. In my mind, it told me that my boss had no confidence in me or my team's abilities without her being directly involved. This made work painful for a long time. I took it personally and figured I would probably lose my job at some point, given her opinion of me.

This went on for months. I was waiting for the axe to fall, but, for some reason, that damn axe wasn't falling on its own. And after she continued this pattern for what seemed like an eternity, I couldn't take it anymore. I couldn't go on with this heavy burden that was going to impact my life at any given moment, so I decided to act first.

Yes, I suppose this move was risky, but I figured just waiting it out was painfully delaying the inevitable. If she didn't need me in this role, then why keep me around? I'll do something where I *can* add value. This was my plan. I was going to tell her how I felt and let her know how her actions harmed me and the team. I naturally assumed, of course, that I would be canned but I was ready. That outcome was far better than me showing up for work every day feeling like I was selling water to whales, which I might add isn't as physically taxing as trying to sell sperm to sperm whales.

Comediology

I requested a meeting with her and she accepted. Despite the foregone conclusion I had reached, I was still very nervous. I hadn't been working with her for a long time and therefore didn't know her well. What I did know, however, did not put me at ease. You see, I had a significant amount of respect for my boss. She had been with the company for many years and was a pillar of its community. Oh yeah, one more thing: the word on the street was "you didn't mess with her." No, seriously. She was decidedly *not* a touchy-feely person. While fair, she was also firm bordering "tough as nails." In fact, once, in a large, public forum, she called "bullshit" on a highly respected Fortune 500 CFO. The CFO, an executive leader of the company, was also her boss's boss. She didn't care. He wasn't making the right decision and he needed to be told. "Bullshit, Greg!" I think is exactly how she phrased it. Outside of a Vin Diesel Movie, you know, the one called *Fast and Furious Bullshit from Greg*, who does that?! She did. She was one of the most authentic people I'd ever met. Once, at a company social event, in front of several hundred people, she got up, grabbed the microphone and belted out Janis Joplin's "Mercedes Benz." Mind you, this was not karaoke night and no one else sang. There was a band playing and they had just finished a song. Without warning, she got up on stage and grabbed the microphone in front of a silently stunned audience. She stared at the crowd for what seemed like an eternity, and then started singing. I'm not sure even Frank Sinatra would ever attempt such a daunting feat. But she would. That's how she rolled. She was a "badass." And here I was going in to have a conversation with her about my "feelings." Seriously? I think Richard Simmons would have better luck serenading the Phantom of the Opera with *The First Time Ever I Saw Your Face*.

She was on a call when I walked into her office. She motioned for me to sit down, and you know what? I did just that. I felt butterflies stir up inside of me as the frustration in her voice heightened, "Yeah, well, I don't care what they think, that's the way the system amortizes!" *Oh crap*, I thought, *what was I thinking?* She won't be able to relate to my feelings at all. Not only was I going to irritate her but she was probably going to laugh at me, too. It was one thing to get fired, but completely another to get laughed at first and then fired, and then laughed at some more. What was I doing?!

She hung up the phone, took a deep breath, and then focused her gaze on me. "So, Chris, what can I do for *you*?" I paused for a moment.

Chris S. Tabish with Kurtis Matthews

The situation was surreal. All our conversations to this point had been very business-centric. We were tech geeks, and these were the types of interactions we had built our relationship on. I had never approached her on anything human. As a result, it was awkward and took me the better part of thirty seconds to steal my vocal cord muscles back from my clinched butt cheeks.

I started in slowly and shakily. "I—I just wanted to have a conversation about how we work together."

"Okay," she replied, "what about it?" As you can see, she wasn't one to mess around with small talk.

I couldn't turn back now; I had gone too far. With a mask of false bravado accompanied by the distinct feeling that I could spontaneously urinate on the carpet at any given moment, I entered the dragon.

"Well," I replied, "I'm not sure if you need me on your team and, quite frankly, I feel like I'm taking advantage of the situation."

"Huh?" she responded. "I'm not sure what you mean by that."

"Well," I continued, "every time me and my team are figuring out a solution, you are always there to jump in and direct traffic. Don't get me wrong, you're great at what you do and your perspective is always valued, but doesn't that make my role sort of redundant?"

And just like being interrupted by the sound of your own flatulence in yoga class, it was out there and there was nothing I could do to take it back. I had jumped out of the hot air balloon tethered to a thin rope, handed her a knife, and, looking up at her, imprudently inquired, "Don't you think we would go higher without all this dead weight?" Ummm . . . what the hell was I thinking again?

She looked up thoughtfully. There was an awkward silence that spanned sufficient time for a woman to conceive, raise a child, and put them through medical school, or to be connected to a live person on the Department of Motor Vehicles customer service line. I wasn't sure how it would happen, but was quite certain the axe would be coming now. After all, this *is* what I had planned.

Her gaze returned to me, but there was an openness about her. If she was a Twinkie, she was now speaking from her creamy, gooey center. "Chris," she said thoughtfully, "designing solutions is what I do. It's what I love. And if I couldn't do that, there would be no point for me to come to work." She continued, "You are doing a great job. You manage the team. Our customers love you and you keep them off my back so I can continue to do what I love. This is what I need you to do and you're doing it. You're not redundant—you enable the team's success."

I must admit, I wasn't prepared for this response. She had just defibrillated me back to life and I was surprisingly elated. I felt joy, connection, and a strong sense of belonging. I had come in to the meeting ignorant and consequently ready to walk. But now, things were different, *completely* different. I'd learned new insights, but, more importantly, I *realized* I had been experiencing pain and personal anguish because I had made it about *me* but it was *never about me*.

I was on cloud nine and remained there for the time that we worked together. My boss and I got along brilliantly as I embraced her working style and her love of solutions. I also could feel that she truly valued me and what I did for the team and the customers. It was like we both completed a puzzle of how we worked together. We each knew where each other fit. As such, we both saw why we were critical to the whole. This eliminated my desire to emulate someone else because we each needed that unique value the other one brought to the table. And to think, I was ready to walk out the door.

This transformation enriched the way she and I worked together and also improved the level of the whole team. Trusting each other enabled us to build a culture of trust for the entire staff. None of this would have happened if I had remained silent and continued "pretending." To reach this breakthrough, I had to be authentic and courageous, and communicate how I truly felt. I had to break through the "norm," the everyday pattern of engagement, and genuinely connect. This was downright frightening, but I had to own it and I'm so grateful that I did. It not only changed the way we worked together but also transformed our relationship. We became friends and are still friends to this day, some twelve years later.

Even if she had booted me out on my ear, I would have concluded the delusion and set myself up for true fulfillment. Yes, it would have been painful for a short time, but much, much shorter than living an illusory, frustrated life forevah and evah and evah.

Sometime after our breakthrough, I learned that she had gone through something very similar. She was working for a boss *she* didn't trust. And,

Chris S. Tabish with Kurtis Matthews

after about a year into the relationship, she told him just that. She literally came out and said, "Boss, I don't trust you." Yes, she told him right there on the spot that his shit stank. And to answer your question, no, she didn't get fired, nor did she get passive-aggressive treatment from him. In fact, what she got was a similar breakthrough. Her boss wanted to understand why she didn't trust him, and from there, they connected authentically. They built a trusted relationship and also remain close to this day.

Communicating in this manner is never easy. It takes courage to look inside of yourself, to allow and acknowledge your feelings and, what's more, communicate them. But who out there is courageous? No, really though. I certainly didn't feel courageous most of the time. In fact, the poet Maya Angelou convinced me that people aren't born courageous, but instead, develop it as if it were a muscle. Angelou states that her mother encouraged her to "develop courage." "You develop it by doing small, courageous things. In the same way that one wouldn't set out to pick up 100 pound bag of rice. If that was one's aim, the person would be advised to pick up a five pound bag, and then a ten pound, and then a 20 pound, and so forth, until one builds up enough muscle to actually pick up 100 pounds. And that's the same way with courage. You develop courage by doing courageous things, small things, but things that cost you some exertion—mental and, I suppose, spiritual exertion."

Whether it's getting up on stage in public and telling a few jokes or communicating what's real to your boss, remember that authenticity is within you and courage can be developed. And, as Maya puts it, "There is no greater agony than bearing an untold story inside you." So now you've been told, now you know. It's time to go forth, prosper, and be a badass.

Comediology

Summary

Congratulations on another chapter read, or at least convincingly flipped through. Seriously, that was some Academy Award performing stuff. Well, you're here anyway, and I'm not going to say anything, so let's review:

1) **If we truly stay connected to what we are understanding, feeling, and communicating, we are being authentic.** People can sense this, and they trust and respect it.

2) **Get in touch with the *feeling* of what you are presenting.** Body language, which reflects your feelings and the unconscious energy you put out there, is what truly makes an impact.

3) **Communicate how you truly feel.** Pretending perpetuates the need to pretend. Be courageous in communicating authentically. It will pay off tenfold. The worst case is you end the delusion and set yourself up for true fulfillment.

4) **Think of courage as a muscle and start developing it.** Start out with small things where the stakes are relatively low and grow it from there. This will gain you tremendous confidence over time.

There's no present. There's only the immediate future and the recent past.

—George Carlin

Presence

I met Pierce Brosnan on my honeymoon. It was awesome. And, at the same time, a total disaster. That said, if it *had* gone well, I wouldn't be able to use it as a story to talk about "how not to be a knucklehead when you meet Pierce Brosnan," now, would I? So yes, I was that knucklehead who "took one for the team." Here goes. . . .

My wife and I got married and honeymooned in Kauai near Anini Beach. We basically lived in that area for a couple of weeks and spent a lot of time getting acquainted with the local lifestyle. One day, we were walking through a parking lot to get some Lappert's Kauai Pie ice Cream, aka frozen crack, when my wife turned to me and said, "Hey, there goes 007."

"Huh?" I replied.

"Yeah," she said. "That was Pierce Brosnan."

Later, she would tell me that she had waited long after he passed us by to reveal his identity because she knows what a celebrity addict I am. Despite the time delay in getting the tip, I couldn't help myself. I was off to find Pierce.

About five minutes later I had a visual on him. He was in the typical spot where you would expect to find famous people—the produce section at a Big Save Market. He had his back turned to me, which only helped reinforce my role as a crazed celebrity stalker. Slowly I approached in a sideways fashion so that if he turned around prematurely, I could easily shift my stance to a casual, "Oh, hey there. Aren't you Pierce Brosnan? Wow, I didn't even notice you amongst all those tomatoes. Ha, ha. By the way, remind me, are they fruits or vegetables?" Ah, the scenarios we play out in our minds. . . .

After a few moments, he did turn around. And now that I had finally reached my preferred stalking location, or PSL as they refer to it in our

TMZ and PopSugar training, I was ready. His casual acknowledgement via head nod was all that I needed to let my celebrity freak flag fly.

"Hey, Pierce," I said, "I love your work, man!" And there it was, my stalking masterpiece. That sentiment was apparently the sole reason I felt compelled to chase down Pierce Brosnan across a parking lot and into a grocery store. It was the full extent of my planning and, as I would soon realize, had exhausted all of my mental faculties as well.

Pierce was amazing. He was gracious and welcoming. He enthusiastically grabbed my hand while vigorously replying, "Hey, thanks man!" Wait . . . what? Wow! I couldn't believe it. I was completely taken aback by his openheartedness and willingness to engage with a potential, and probably actual, celebrity nut. Truth be told, I was expecting the same reaction I got from Sigourney Weaver when I held the door open for her at a Malibu Starbucks. I was completely awestruck and googly-eyed while I held the door. She, on the other hand, was not so enchanted and looked at me with a facial expression that screamed, "Get away from me—you smell like Martha Stewart's prison mattress."

Pierce was shaking my hand for what seemed like an eternity. I didn't know what to do with all this attention from one of the most famous persons in the world. And with my reserves emptied, I spontaneously transformed into Homer Simpson—"celebrity shaking hand, must walk away before stupid leaves tongue." I'm a natural conversationalist, I love talking to people. But in that moment, I truly couldn't put two words together to save my life.

I stood there in a stupor while Pierce gently swayed my hand back and forth like a good son visiting his senile grandfather. A moment passed, then another, and then another still. This was becoming too weird. He was quite good at this and I realized he must have had a lot of experience with elderly or heavily sedated fans. That said, I felt sorry for Pierce. He had kindly reached out to connect with an admirer, but now was permanently attached to a human slot machine that, unfortunately for him, only paid out with Kaua'i Pie Ice cream breath and awe-induced slobber—I mean, mouth-crying.

I couldn't keep doing this. After all, he had his own life to live, didn't he? Perhaps he could die another day (really, Chris, really?). I released my grasp and without saying a word, turned around and beelined it out the

Comediology

door. No "goodbye," no "nice to meet you." Nothing. That was apparently just way too high of an expectation of myself at the time or, as I would prefer to remember it, "I'm just cool like that." I was grateful to have met Pierce, but had decided it was now time to return to a simpler life. A life I could find with the friendly, furry faces on *Sesame Street*, where, once again, I would be taught the ways of letters and how they could be put together to form words and, perhaps someday with practice, exercise, and a healthy diet, sentences.

After this embarrassing event transpired, I immediately turned to my good friend Denial. After all, he had been very effective in the past at proving that he was much more than a mere river in Africa. At times when I was a complete jackass, Denial would always be there to offer me sanctuary and justification. "Nobody saw your ultraviolet night light, aka, string of toilet paper, straggling from the butt of your jeans at the dance club," he would argue. "And if they did, they were probably just jealous of you starting a new fashion trend. Or, perhaps they assumed it was for good luck like one of those dragons at a Chinese New Year's Parade." While Denial was usually quite effective at comforting me, I slowly began to realize he could offer no sanctuary in this situation. You see, I was talking to Pierce Brosnan. He was a famous actor, so how could he possibly relate to such an "ordinary Joe" in me? Yet, here he was at a very ordinary supermarket. And he was picking out ordinary produce. Although in hindsight, those tomatoes were really in season.

Pierce was also very welcoming. In fact, the interaction with Pierce was one of the warmest receptions I've ever had from a total stranger, much less a movie star. This led me to seek counsel from my fair-weather friend, Reflection. He was a no-holds-barred kind of guy who dwelled in fact and logic without regard for my feelings. So, while he certainly was not as likeable, he did offer some keen insights. And while I still don't agree with him that my body odor isn't to just die for, he helped shed some light on this situation. He helped me understand that the real problem wasn't the situation. The real problem was me. I wasn't being present. I wasn't in the moment. I was interacting with something that I had built up in my mind that wasn't reality.

After realizing the issue, it was easy to mentally correct the situation. I would simply hop in the DeLorean, go back to 1985, and break out some

Chris S. Tabish with Kurtis Matthews

"Johnny B. Goode." Then I head back to the Big Save Market in 2004 to chat it up with Pierce. Only this time, I'm present. I find that common ground. After all, I'm sure we've both had to deal with airplane flatulence on more than one occasion. We become fast friends and Pierce invites me over for some totally amazing tomato stew and Valium.

Then I realize, of course, that I've fallen into the trap—again! I'm not being present right here, right now. You only get *one chance* to be present in *this* moment. Then, you get a gazillion more chances to be present in every subsequent moment going forward. But here's the thing: you can only be present in the moment you're in, *right now*. My advice to you, and to me, in my best Jersey Mafia boss voice, is this: "Don't blow it, heh?"

Be here, right now. Don't let your mind or situation run away like some crazy train. . . . All aboard! Hahahahahahahaaaa! Ay ay-ay-ay-ay-ay-ay. Wow, thanks again, Ozzy, for helping me drive this one home. Be here, right now. Take it in and just be you. Realistically, what are you going to solve by being in another time or place? Moreover, when have you ever done anything in the past or the future? Let it go. Come back to here. Come back to now. And yes, speaking from experience, even if that means you're a lobotomized Homer Simpson in front of a demigod. The only way through it is to go *through* it. So, commit completely and give yourself wholly to the present moment. This is your best bet for fulfillment via going through the adventure, facing adversity, falling in love, gaining perspective and enjoying the ride.

The First Time

It's always entertaining to see new comedians start out. It's totally gross and completely delicious at the same time. It's gross because it's a train wreck and you're witnessing a person go through a very painful, public experience. On the other hand, it's delicious because it's a train wreck and you're witnessing a person go through a very painful, public experience.

First-timers are an interesting bunch. They're so sure that they're going to be the next thing. Yet simultaneously, they desperately want to be liked by everyone. Of course, they're funny. After all, didn't their mom and best friend's little sister laugh hysterically when they told the one about the hurdler that walked into a "bar"? (Get it, "bar"? I mean seriously, people, this is good stuff.) They're going to kill on stage. Shortly thereafter, they'll

Comediology

be signing their comedian contract, probably by Tuesday. You know, just to work out the detailed terms such as flying first class, front-row seats for Mama at *The Kimmel Show*, and absolutely no olives on their backstage churros.

Like many things in life, the reality of the situation tends to be slightly, or in this case, drastically, different than what was imagined. In reality, the host announces the beginning comedian's name and they get up on stage. That part is the same. It's everything that happens *from* that point forward that's completely different than how they imagined it. For starters, there are bright lights blazing into their eyes. There is a row of people just looking at them, evaluating them, wondering what they're about. "Hmmm . . . that's new," they think. They reach for the microphone. They start to speak and hear a quiver in their voice that positively wasn't there when they had performed it in their head on *The Tonight Show*. They tell their first joke but rush the timing. The audience doesn't laugh. Well, more accurately, they start to chuckle. But our beginning comedian, aka Smokey The Hacky Bear, stomps all over their laughter with the next joke before it can come to life.

Rapidly, our comedian realizes he's not connecting with the audience. And a new guest star spontaneously appears on stage—awkwardness. Our beginner doesn't know what to do. The only safety line he has is his material, and that's clearly not helping him. It's difficult enough to remain on stage delivering jokes that aren't funny; thinking of switching up the plan and going off script is completely out of the question. After all, he reflects, sounding just like a frog who jumped into cool water that is now boiling hot, "What if it becomes weird?"

He holds on for dear life while rapidly regurgitating his material like a livestock auctioneer. "Non-funny joke number twelve, do I hear a laugh? Do I hear a laugh? No laugh. Going once, going twice. Okay, and we're on to joke thirteen. Do I hear a laugh from anyone? Anyone? Anyone got a laugh for the big thirteen? No one? No one? Okay, moving onto non-funny joke number fourteen. . . ." Like an endless spray of demonic, green goop, the bad jokes keep coming while the discomfort increases.

Alas, the monotony is broken when an audience member makes a comment. Our beginner comedian has no idea what was said. He can't hear anything. After all, his biology is convinced that the end is near;

consequently, he now considers that his only defense may be that of an opossum; immediately fall into a coma-like state and lay motionless on the stage until the audience leaves. *Why is someone making a comment?* he thinks. *Hopefully they'll just stop if ignored.* Nope. They make another comment and people laugh. *Oh my God*, he realizes, *they're laughing at him more than me!*

Before his time on stage, he felt his comedy was akin to a sweet pastry that everyone would simply adore. But, then, on stage for the first time and in a flash of a moment, this moment, he realizes that his comedic pastry is merely a plain doughnut and his act is the center. His act would be significantly more marketable and palatable if just one thing were removed—him.. His friends humiliate him further by consoling him: "Hey man, you got up there in front of everyone, you know. That's huge, bro."

At least *I think* that's what they said to me.

If this were a math or science exam, our beginning comedian would have received an A+. He had studied diligently and knew the material completely. Simply put, it's not such an exam. But we can't be too hard on our comedian. After all, in school, he, along with all of us, had been trained to prepare for life by referencing the past. Just look at every test we've ever taken. What have we read? What has the instructor told us? What did he say was going to be on the quiz?

There are two problems with this approach. First, it's boring. Second, and more importantly, it doesn't help us with stand-up comedy, much less life. You can't connect with a person, much less an audience, by regurgitating the past. Well, okay, I mean *besides* Mr. Johnson's seventh-grade textbook recitals. Admittedly, I still reverberate with orgasmic wonder every time I think about the signing of the Declaration of Independence.

We are dynamic, multidimensional beings that feed off many channels of interaction. What are you saying? Where are you looking? What is your body language? Why is your voice inflecting? Are you personally connected to the material? Are you engaging with me? Did you use a smiley face or add an "LOL"? Do you want my body and think I'm sexy? These, and many others like them, are the questions we're looking to answer while interacting. It's what we need to connect. And here's the thing: it can never be completely scripted. No matter how meticulously you plan, no

Comediology

two audiences are exactly alike. Therefore, you need a different approach. *You need to be present.*

You can't teach someone how to be present with *words*. You must get them to experience how presence *feels*. Our comedy instructor Kurtis was keenly aware of this. And while seemingly cruel, he was quite effective at waking people up in this regard. His approach was ingenious. He would simply unleash hell on a beginner's act until they were present and "in the room" with the audience.

It went something like this. Whenever a beginner was aimlessly spewing off material, Kurtis would spontaneously insert himself as part of their act. Like a lunatic late for a train that was never going to arrive, he would get up and start pacing in front of the stage between the comedian and the audience. Most of the time, the beginner would be confused and unsure of what to do. All they wanted, of course, was to desperately finish their act free of awkwardness.

Sometimes this interruption woke the comedian up. But most of the time, it didn't. At least not the first sixty times. If they started on their next joke without acknowledging the situation, they would be painstakingly interrupted by Kurtis. He would make a noise like an injured donkey teaching aerobics: "Derrrrrrrr!" Everyone in the room would laugh. Everyone, that is, except for the comedian on stage. Like a cat stuck in a tree wanting to get down but fearful of the strange, hairy-knuckled beast reaching up to get them, they mindlessly ventured further into trouble. The comedian wouldn't stop, wouldn't even pause, but just kept awkwardly plowing ahead with their memorized material.

Next joke, same thing—the beginner would start talking and Kurtis would spout out off again: "Deeeeee!" It was crazy how this situation kept perpetuating itself. It was as if the comedian was used to performing for Sloth from the movie *Goonies*, and being interrupted with baboon-like mantras was all in a day's work. It became abundantly apparent to me how strong our instinct is to frantically grasp for a script when life calls for us to simply be present.

With the act finally over, Kurtis would sit down and inquire, "So. Didn't you see me?"

The response from our bewildered and embarrassed comedian was often, "Well, yeah."

Chris S. Tabish with Kurtis Matthews

"Then why didn't you acknowledge me?" Kurtis asked as he waited for the inevitable and abundantly underwhelming response of, "Ummm . . . I dunno."

Fortunately, I do know, because sadly, I've been there myself. The comedian didn't acknowledge the instructor because he simply was not present. He was in a world where you signed up for comedy and then you delivered a monologue and then everyone clapped and you got rich and famous. He was living in La La Land—with a lucrative comedy career complete with millions of dollars, fame, and ultimately a Pirates of the Caribbean amusement park ride that went in his backyard right between the Weber Genesis Grill and his new set of Lawn Jarts—but not in the present moment. He had signed up for comedy, not Kurtis, the crazy, invisible train catcher, pacing back and forth in front of him while he performed. And he was sure that, if continually ignored, Kurtis would just go away and he could resume his comedy world as he had envisioned it. But here's the thing: you can't pick and choose which reactions you want—*ever*. You can't say, oh, yes, "Giggling Martha" in the front row is a keeper, but go ahead and remove Frank of the "sweaty and opinionated."

As a comedian, you're out there in the unpredictable ocean where anything can happen. Yes, you've practiced swimming and you've prudently mapped out a plan, but the reality is that you have control of exactly *nothing* past your big toe. As you start to swim, along comes a wave and it's huge. As always in life, you have options. One option is that you just ignore it, hoping it will go away. Oh, and I hope you like eating California rolls through your nasal cavity.

Another, more preferred option, is that you open yourself up to the present moment. You acknowledge the wave. As such, you don't ignore it and you don't run away, but instead, you turn your body around to *embrace* it. You immediately feel the shift. No longer are you going against the wave *fearing* it, but instead you feel yourself at one with the wave. You pick up speed and start gliding atop it. You feel a rush of excitement and pure ecstasy as you race across the ocean's surface.

This is what happens when you are present, and you embrace the now. Things or events that initially present themselves as intimidating forces transform themselves into catalysts to incredibly amazing experiences. There are many benefits to doing this. First, and most obvious, you don't get slammed by the wave and thus avoid becoming worse off than where you started. Second, by embracing and riding the wave, you feel alive, joyful, even inspired, and so are better off than where you started. Third, as you ride, or attempt to ride, the wave, you are learning and growing, realizing what approach works and what does not. And finally, you become the master of your destiny. As such, you are increasing your confidence because you are *standing up to life*, taking on the challenge and not running away. Yes, it's true, you may fall by embracing the wave. But you've got nothing to lose because ignoring it would have gotten you an ass-kicking anyway.

Embrace the now. Be present. Go off script. Take on that wave and you'll start to realize and unlock the tremendous potential within you.

Comediology

August 28, 1963. Martin Luther King Jr. had taken the stage at the Lincoln Memorial in Washington, DC, to address an audience of more than 250,000 civil rights supporters. In anticipation of this, King had prepared a script. In fact, he had drafted several scripts. The original speech title was something you've probably never heard of before—"Normalcy, Never Again." And although that title didn't stick, ironically, it did an outstanding job of living up to its name.

The speech that King was to give was part of the "March on Washington for Jobs and Freedom," one of the largest political rallies for human rights in the country's history. People had come from every corner of the United States. The turnout was staggering when you consider that, at the time, there was no Facebook, Evite, LinkedIn, or even cell phones. As it turns out, back in those days, people *actually talked* to other people.

Although King was a master public speaker and thus a master preparer, just twelve hours before his speech he wasn't exactly sure what he was going to say. And evidently following my "How To Get Through College 101" course, he didn't finish writing the speech until few hours before dawn— *the day of the event*!

When the moment arrived for King to talk, he did what any one of us would do in front of a crowd of 250,000, besides resisting the strong urge to spontaneously urinate. He stuck to the script. And, in so doing, he was giving a good speech; in fact, it was a *really* good speech. The speech was

Chris S. Tabish with Kurtis Matthews

thought provoking. It was influential. It was also well researched, referring to Lincoln's Gettysburg Address, the Declaration of Independence, the Emancipation Proclamation, and even the Constitution—even more impressive at a time when there was no Google and thus no means to instantly query and retrieve historical data. On the positive side, there was no Siri to completely irritate the bejesus out of him either.

So, once again, the speech was impressive. However, despite all this goodness, it was simply not cutting the mustard for everyone. And by everyone, I mean Mahalia.

Mahalia Jackson was a gospel singer commonly referred to as "the Queen of Gospel." Where King had a gift for moving people through speech, Mahalia's gift was her voice. She used it to inspire people through the civil rights movement. She was no stranger to King and often appeared with him, singing before his speeches. And she was there on this historic day.

Although King had been preaching about dreams since 1960, the script in his hand did not contain the words "I have a dream." So, it's a good thing that Mahalia was nearby. She had listened to his earlier "dream" speeches. She knew the difference between "scripted King" and "bare your soul to the masses" King. And she was going to make sure the latter was brought to the stage.

Toward the end of his speech, Mahalia prompted King, "Tell them about the dream, Martin." The provocation had its desired effect. King, who had been following the script to that point, spontaneously departed from it. His subsequent words were improvised, spoken from a place of heart and total presence. So much so that his wife, Coretta Scott King, remarked that his words flowed "from some higher place." As he spoke from this place, he punctuated his points with "I have a dream"—which, of course, is how we recognize the speech to this day.

For anyone that has listened to the speech, you know that it's moving. The words connect, yes, but the emotion is palpable, and it completely draws you in. You hang on every word and you can feel King's belief and conviction through his voice and his body language. It's amazing that even though he goes off script, you never hear an "umm" or "uhh" but just his eloquent words delivering very effective sentences. This is because King was not anxious, not rushed; he was simply in the moment, letting his essence flow.

Comediology

To do this in front of such a large crowd at such a monumental event, King had to let go of his script, his prepared research and material, and completely trust in himself. He had to trust that his presence and conviction in his beliefs would have a greater impact than any script he had so diligently prepared. And he was right.

In the wake of his monumental speech, King was named *Time* magazine's "Man of The Year" two years in a row. He also became the youngest person ever to receive the Nobel Peace Prize. His speech lives on to this day. In a 1999 poll of Scholars of Public Address, it ranked as the top American speech of the twentieth century.

King's speech was the height of challenge and expectation. It was also the peak of delivery. Yes, King did the work he needed to do in preparing through research and numerous drafts. But, just as important, if not more so, he trusted himself to go off script and be present with his audience. This is what I believe, more than anything else, catapulted King's speech to greatness.

Have you ever been presenting and knew you needed to change things up from what you had prepared, but instead went right on going? I know I have. I did so because I was too frightened to stray from the script. Two things locked me into my prepared material. One is the fear of the unknown. The other was not trusting myself.

Fear of the unknown

We find safety in what we've prepared. We generally think of a prepared speech as if it's a gift-wrapped package we merely need to hand over or "administer" to an audience. But this is not reality. It's easier to comprehend this concept when you think about doing anything in the physical world that requires both preparation and, subsequently, connection.

For example, I recently put up a fence around my yard. After all, precautions must be made lest someone break in and take a swim in my algae-filled, above-ground pool. It was one thing to prepare for this process. It was completely another thing to connect it to my property. During preparation, for instance, I had to plan the fence pattern, purchase the lumber, ready the tools, purchase drugs for the contractor, and so on. After all this was done, conceptually speaking, it was simply a matter of placing the lumber in the places I had planned, right? Wrong.

Chris S. Tabish with Kurtis Matthews

During the process, molehills, stubborn terrain, rocks, and doggie dingleberries all obstructed my original plan. There were constant distractions as well—my neighbor was being a real dingleberry himself. Well, let's be honest, he's always a dingleberry; he just happened to be home on that particular day and was of the opinion that neighborly conversation was most preferred while holding a towel and wearing a thong. Moreover, my wife and kids had their own agendas, too. Why they actually wanted to engage with me as a human being on that day, I'll never know. Couldn't they see that I had dropped all identity and responsibilities of being a husband and father to being the Karate Kid, waxing on and off, for the next six hours? Here's the thing: to successfully connect the wood to my property, I had to be present in recognizing obstacles, and had to be open to adjusting my plans accordingly.

Presenting to a live audience is no different. Preparation should be thought of as just that—preparation. Words are written and rehearsed and that's necessary. However, the whole point of presenting in front of the audience is to *connect* yourself and your material *with* your audience. And the process of preparing doesn't do this.

Hopefully you have a good idea of the audience's point of view while you are preparing, as it is critical in any public speaking event to "know thy audience." However, like the fence example, audiences are made up of people with their own set of personal dramas—molehills, stubborn terrain, and rocks. And yes, it's true—some are just dingleberries. All of this will undoubtedly affect how they perceive you and your material. Your preparation equips you with material, but it's done in a figurative vacuum. Unless, of course, someone out there is literally preparing their speeches in a vacuum . . . weird. Your audience is a dynamic entity. Therefore, you will need to be open, perceptive, and ready to adjust. In other words, you will need to be present.

Trusting yourself

Clinging on to your material is like holding onto the rails while ice skating. While you may not fall, you're certainly not going to learn much, and you definitely won't amaze anyone, including yourself.

Just like building the fence, it's not easy diverting from a plan. You're not sure what's going to come up or how you're going to deal with it when

Comediology

it does. It's like working with a recipe. Perhaps you've started it and then things went wrong. You used salted tomatoes when it called for unsalted, and you threw in a silo of corn when it only called for a teaspoon. Dude! You tried to get back on script by adding in more of everything else, but to no avail. The path you're on clearly isn't working, but straying is still frightening. After all, you're no chef and you've never done this kind of thing from scratch before. So, it's better, you think, to have a mediocre meal than set the oven on fire.

But that's where we don't give ourselves enough credit and, consequently, opportunity. To differentiate ourselves in *anything* we must be original. To be original, we must go off script. *Your dreams won't come true by following directions.* Shit, mind you, is going to happen. You're not going to make the recipe like everyone else. So what? Who ever discovered anything new by knowing what the hell they were doing the whole time?! By going off script, you're going to learn something, and it may just be fantastic and awesome. You've got taste buds and fingers, right? So, jump in! Have fun, be present, and go after it! If you truly embrace this, not only will you have a great time, but this, my friends, is where the miracles happen.

Many amazing discoveries came about because people completely mucked up their recipes. Instead of throwing in the towel, however, they stayed present, trusted in themselves, and continued the off-script adventure. Just look at some of the wonderful things that were discovered by accident. Play-Doh was supposed to be wallpaper cleaner. (By the way, wasn't that whole point of wallpaper was so you didn't ever have to clean your walls again?) Potato chips were supposed to be French fries until a patron sent them back calling them "undercooked," which caused the chef to retaliate and over-fry and -salt them. And then blame it on the French. Corn Flakes were supposed to be easily digestible bread for patients until one of the Kellogg brothers boiled the wheat for several hours longer than intended—oopsie. Although I have to believe this one was accompanied by some good marketing. "Overcooked, you say? No, Jude . . . ha, ha, this is a new and improved recipe. In fact, it took us *several* hours longer to make it this way. You do . . . like it . . . don't you?"

The Slinky was supposed to be a spring that would stabilize and support sensitive instruments on naval ships. Okay, what?! "We've got Slinkys, North Korea, so back the !#!@ off or we'll use them! And if that

Chris S. Tabish with Kurtis Matthews

doesn't work, we'll unleash our Ninja Turtle Dolls!" Popsicles were a fruit-flavored drink with a stir stick that was accidently left out one night in the freezing cold. Chocolate chip cookies were supposed to be Butter Drop Do cookies until Ruth Wakefield ran out of baker's chocolate. In a panic, she broke up a bar of Nestlé's semisweet chocolate into tiny chips, making the first batch of what would later be known as the reason every American is slightly overweight. And the list goes on. Even this book was originally supposed to be a rock concert at Madison Square Garden for 50,000 raving fans. But I never got an agent and, contrary to every other musician out there, I refused to learn another instrument. What can I say? The air guitar and jug band just made sense to me.

Even the Wright Brothers, who intentionally set out to create a flying machine, had no clue what they were doing at first. To their credit, they let go of the rails early on. Realizing that the information they needed was not documented, they went off script and jumped in to learn details never captured before with pen and paper. They did this by spending time watching birds fly. Yes, that's right, watching birds fly! Talk about trusting yourself—"Yeah, sorry, I won't be at work for a while. I'm going down to the beach to watch birds fly for the next two months or so."

You've got to trust yourself to go there. You've got to believe that your presence is enough to handle the situations as they come up. Your mind, while useful for following directions and constantly inquiring if you've turned the stove off, could not keep you alive for more than five minutes. Heart rate, blood flow, breathing, sweating, digesting—even things like intuition and feelings. These all come from your being. There is more intelligence within us than we could ever consciously know. By being present, we turn down the mind and turn up our being.

Whether it be a speech, project, meeting, conversation, or anything else, you never know when you will get the comedian instructors of the world pacing in front of you making weird donkey noises. You must be prepared. And the best way you can be prepared is to be present. When you're present, you're not thinking about what you *should* be saying because that's what the presentation states or that's what your boss thinks. Likewise, you're not thinking about tomorrow and all the potential "what if" scenarios that could ensue if you don't disseminate your information properly. Put simply, *you aren't living in fear.* You are living in the current

Comediology

moment. Everything is real time. There is no judgment. There is only active listening and authentic response. When you are responding out of fear, you are playing not to lose. When you are present, you are playing to win.

By being present, if there is an elephant on the table, akin to the crazy instructor walking in front of the stage, you'll deal with it, together with your audience. You'll walk away aligned and probably have fun doing it. Even if you disagree, you'll both acknowledge what's there. That puts you much further ahead than if you'd gone on blindly regurgitating.

In business, like in stand-up comedy, we can't pick and choose which elements we want to engage in our work life. In fact, *most* of the things we interact with in our career are out of our control—the crazy people, the venues, the Wi-Fi reception, more crazy people, the laptop that won't project, the crazy people's relatives, and so forth.

Therefore, while we must be prepared, we must be open to interacting with our environment in the present moment. *You can't do things in the past. You can't do things in the future.* You can only affect change here and now. Therefore be here. Now. Be present and live in the land of possibilities.

Summary

In short, not everything you do is going to get you fame and glory. You might even get gonged and have to exit stage left. But don't let that stop you from trying. Some of what you thought were your greatest defeats can turn out to be your greatest victories. You never know. Here goes the rest. . . .

1) **Preparation and presentation are two completely separate things:** Preparation is necessary to know your message and even understand your audience, but it won't *connect* you with your audience. The best way to connect yourself and your material with your audience is to be *present* with them.

2) **Prepare for the unexpected.** Have a script and know it. But when presenting, watch for the cues and be present enough to go off script when necessary.

3) **Trust in your presence and that your essence will have a greater impact than merely regurgitating what you prepared.** Go there. Your courage and abilities will grow the more often you do this, but you've got to take that first step.

4) **Your dreams won't come true by following directions.** To differentiate yourself in anything, you must be original. To be original, you must be present and open to opportunities.

5) **Make the choice to stop "playing not to lose" and "play to win."**

Behind every great man is a woman rolling her eyes.

—Jim Carrey

Competition versus Creation

When I started out doing stand-up comedy, I would watch the other comedians. They fell into three categories: (1) they were funny, (2) they were really funny, or (3) they made me look like I was about to get my own comedy special. The last was super-hard to do, by the way. Bless those newbies. I would categorize them because I was evaluating them. I would observe their set and listen intently for the audience's reaction. I wasn't "enjoying" the other comedian's acts, mind you. I was "judging" them and specifically assessing their merits as compared to my act.

You see, at the time, I was being what the Village People called an "idiot." More specifically, I was living under the delusion that I and my fellow comedians were in a competition. Don't ask me why. Maybe I stood too close to the microwave during my "Lynn Wilson Burrito" phase. Note that some of you born after the invention of the wheel may refer to it as the "Cup O' Noodles" phase. Regardless, for me it was a competition, but only in *my* mind. I mean, no one was ever announced a winner. No one got a trophy. Hell, no one even got a Family Feud Board Game as a consolation prize. Ah, but one can still dream.

When I was judging the other comedian's acts, my evaluation criteria were simple. If I could make the audience laugh more than the other comedians who were also on stage that night, I was (in my best Borat) great success! Otherwise, I was a total and complete failure. I would use this barometer to compare myself to every other comedian who performed that night. It didn't matter if the other comedian was a fellow beginner or twenty-year veteran of comedy. If they got more laughs, they were decidedly, at least in my mind, the winner. And I was the comedic loser. And just like Don Music from *Sesame Street*, I would bang my head against the microphone, screaming, "I'll nevah make them laugh! NEVAH!!!" If this continued, I feared I would be shunned from the community and destined to live as a boring professional. I would need to change my name to Donald J. Herberrocker, Accounting. I would drown myself in Excel spreadsheets, wear sweater vests in July, and carry around a partially hydrated handkerchief at all times.

It was painful. I wasn't enjoying myself. And I wasn't enjoying any of the acts, including mine. I wasn't even recognizing and giving myself credit for being courageous enough to do what I was doing, much less acknowledging that it was a process and took time to cultivate. Consequently, I was defensive. After all, in my mind, I sucked. I wasn't happy with myself. How could I be sincerely happy for others who succeeded, when, at least by my gorilla math, it was at my own expense? I would even do really dumb stuff like not laugh at their jokes, just to influence the outcome. Yes, I *really* did that, and yes, I apparently just wrote it down so now everyone knows that I *really* did that. Can you imagine that? Everyone is sitting around having a great time laughing at a comedian and I'm sitting over in the corner all pouted up like John McEnroe: "You can't be serious, man. YOU CANNOT BE SERIOUS! That joke was not funny! Non-humorous words flew up! It was clearly not funny! You guys are the absolute pits of the world . . . and I will not, I repeat, NOT be laughing."

In retrospect, why didn't I just go into beauty pageants?

Since that time, I've reflected deeply upon my thoughts and behavior. I've read age-old adages and contemplated the topic intensely. And, after much spiritual and cerebral introspection, I've come to the profound conclusion that I was plagued with what is referred to in Latin as "asinorum" or, more commonly known as, being a "jackass."

Being a jackass is not fun or fulfilling, and it's no way to live life. It gets tiring being skeptical, bitter, and judgmental. And it's no way to expand your Amway pyramid. I couldn't be sincerely happy for any other person's success because I was too busy living in fear of how it might eclipse my own. And if you're not happy with your own success and can't be happy with anyone else's, when *will* you be happy? Oh yeah, well, I mean besides *after* you eat that last pint of Ben and Jerry's.

I was living in a competitive world with an outside-in perspective. When you do this, it's difficult, if not impossible, to create. I was chasing and reacting to what I saw, not creating. I was comparing myself to others and found myself fixated on trying to do the same things they did. I would,

Comediology

of course, try to do it funnier than how they did it, but this was hard to do. After all, mine was a carbon copy whereas theirs was the original.

I was playing a game of "whack-a-mole," trying to emulate every other good act I saw. Thus, my skillset was capped to whatever act I could see. Through this method, I limited myself to being somewhere in the range of "as good as" or, more often than not, "worse" than my competitors. After all, how could I differentiate when they were my target? Even if I was funny and had a good night of performing, I was not distinguishable from the other comedians. How could I be, when I was emulating them?

It took time to realize this was not the path to fulfillment. It took even more time to admit it to myself. And it took courage to give myself permission to explore what potentially *could* be the path—creation.

Authentic creation, exclusive of competition, is a scary place to enter. There are no guard rails. You can't get there being fixated on what others are doing. By definition, it is bringing something into existence outside the norm. There is no voice in your head to assure you that, "hey, what you're doing is totally normal and like everyone else." The reality is just the opposite. With creativity, you are doing things different from *everyone else.*

That said, to stand out in the crowd—to tap into your comedic gift— you *need* to be different from everyone else. Think about every amazing comedian out there. They have a different act, a different point of view, a different "funny." Sam Kinison was brilliant but very different from Robin Williams, who was very different than Jerry Seinfeld, and so on. If Kinison had tried to do the multiple personalities of Robin Williams, it would have been lackluster at best. Likewise, you wouldn't have been able to slow Robin Williams down long enough to do the insightful observations of Jerry Seinfeld. And I can't imagine Jerry Seinfeld doing a Kinison and screaming out at the top of his lungs, "You don't even speak English, how the *$%# did you get this job?! Ahhh!! Ahhh! And by the way, what's the deal with carrots?!"

If they had been competitive copycats, the originality within them never would have come out. They would have been reduced to an unauthentic version of themselves, a facsimile of someone else. And sadly, we would have been deprived of their authentic gift of comedy.

I was slowly realizing this concept over time. And, believe me, it does take time. You see, traditionally, our society has told us to "follow the rules" to get rewarded. We point out other people's successes and then do our best to "follow in their footsteps" because, after all, "great minds think alike," right? And then you see a truly differentiated success and think, "Wow, they're doing it. It's unique and it's wonderful. Why didn't I follow *my* instinct like them instead of following everyone else?" Remember this. And this is important. You must reprogram your thinking. All of the societal guidance you've received in terms of "fitting in" is great for garden parties, Santa's elves, or being buried in the sweet part of the cemetery. But as it pertains to your direction in life, it's about as useful as a dentist with *Tyrannosaurus rex* hands.

Unlike competition, which is grounded in the achievements of your competitors, creation has no limits, no boundaries. Emulating others or, God forbid, "following the rules," pales in comparison to creation. "I'll be as great as Tina Fey but no better" said absolutely no one we've ever heard of on *The Tonight Show*.

Creating from what is inside your soul and what your mind can imagine is boundless. It is a gift if you embrace it. It will lead you to great adventures and push you to new heights you never dreamed of or thought possible before. If you repress it, however, it will remain a source of frustration, a continual burden, a constant regret like that gum you swallowed when you were seven—and yes, it's still being digested. By stuffing your gift, you shortchange *yourself* by not experiencing the exhilaration of living through your creativity. Moreover, you shortchange *everyone else* by not letting them experience your creation.

Do you think it's ridiculous to think that by not embracing your creativity, you are depriving others? Okay, then, let's reverse the scenario; as with many things in life, it's easier to see outside of yourself. What if *your* favorite movie, painting, song, app, book, commercial, game, gadget, speech, play, musical, invention, joke, dance, documentary, act, video, drawing, picture, show, or episode simply never existed?

That's right. The movie line that you and your friend always laugh about, the song that you play to get inspired before a workout, the play that has become a holiday tradition for your family and, alas, the joke that you find hysterical but refuse to laugh at because your spouse is sitting next to you. Yes, this is what we're talking about. How many times have those creations lifted us from our emotional abyss? How many times have they

Comediology

given us joy and fulfillment? How often have they gotten us through a dreadful Monday morning? How many times have they connected us with other people, thereby initiating or deepening our relationships?

Dammit, Jim! Don't you see it? *This is the magic of life*! We're talking *Game of* !#@! *Thrones* here, people! And if those creators had never embraced their creativity, they would have unknowingly deprived our lives. So, once again, if *you* don't embrace *your* creativity, *you* will deprive *yourself* and *everyone else*. Don't make me use another *italic word* here, people! Seriously, don't do this. It's dumb. We need you. We need your creativity. Signed, The Entire Human @#!%ing Race.

Whereas competition stems from judging people and events *outside of you*, creativity is something that bubbles up from *within you*. Whereas competition will make you bitter, creativity fulfills you. It feels so good when you've created something original that came uniquely from you. Compare that triumphant feeling to "not being as funny as Judy." Once you comprehend this, you begin to realize that you are in competition with no one. Because no one else can be you and you cannot be anyone else. And Judy really isn't that funny anyway when you think about it.

The choice for me was simple. I could continue hating on everyone else's success and grow old and bitter faster than my years. Or, I could experience true fulfillment through focusing on my original creations and supporting others focusing on theirs. In other words, I could become a thoughtful and caring human being.

The bigger show

When I first got up on stage as a beginner, I didn't realize that there was a "bigger show." As often is the case with life, when you are small, you think small—or is it the other way around? I naïvely thought that a show was simply a conglomerate of disparate comedians clomped together. However, as I advanced, I realized that there was a "connectedness" to it all. And, as is the case with things that are connected, anything that influences an individual part, impacts the whole. It's true—just ask my digestive tract.

If you go to a movie and it is hysterical for the first thirty minutes, it puts you in a mood to laugh for the rest of the movie. If something funny happens at minute 31, you're already laughing and therefore more prone

Chris S. Tabish with Kurtis Matthews

to laugh. Conversely, if the movie is boring for the first thirty minutes and something funny happens at minute 31, you're like, "Seriously, Dominos, thirty minutes is up, where've you been?!" At that point, it feels like a chore to start the laughing engine. If it's really funny, you might giggle or chuckle a bit, but it won't be the same as if you'd been laughing the entire time. And you certainly wouldn't be satisfied going to a movie with only a few funny minutes of funny. You want a *full movie* of funny.

Likewise, in comedy, if the comedians who go before you put on a great show and get the people laughing, your job is much, *much* easier. It's like the saying goes: "In a strong wind, even the turkeys fly." The bearings have been oiled, the skids greased, and people are ready to laugh. This is exactly why they have warm-up acts in comedy. Therefore, as a comedian, other than being funny yourself, one of the best opportunities to get laughs from the audience is to make sure that the comedians *before* you get big laughs.

This was the opposite of my previous reptilian-brain conclusion. After all, I was secretly (well, now publicly, I guess—hi there, world) hoping that the people before me would bomb. Then, I would get up on stage and "save the day." The people would realize how funny *I* was, relative to the other, loser comedians, cheer nonstop, then invite me on to *The Late Show*. Please note that this embarrassing fantasy came before I hit comedic puberty.

Now, let's compare the dream to reality. If the people bombed before me, I would get up on stage. I would make eye contact with a bunch of now disinterested people, and they would give me the expression like, "Oh great, another one." This is assuming of course that they hadn't already headed for the door. How's that for a vote of confidence?

Once you've disinterested or irritated an audience, it's challenging to get their positive emotions back. Anyone who has peed on the proverbial relationship carpet knows this. (Well, now that I think about it, I suppose *literally* peeing on a carpet would also have the same effect.) Maybe you forgot an anniversary. Maybe you skipped a birthday. Or perhaps you flushed the contents of their cat's litter box down their fourth-floor condominium toilet with the cat still in it. Either way, we've all been there, right? Wait, where are you going?

By the way, just a quick departure as I want to, once again, apologize to all the tenants that lived in the Lakeside San Francisco apartment building.

Comediology

I'm really, truly sorry for transforming your homes into the *SS Kitty Shit Box* during the Memorial Day weekend of 2000. You see, I've never owned a cat before and therefore wasn't fully versed on the concept of kitty litter. I was not aware, for example, that kitty litter spontaneously, and quite rapidly I might add, transforms into a cemented plug when a full box of it is flushed down the toilet. Who knew? Furthermore, I was not conscious of the fact that this plug can block the entire drainage system of a fifty-unit building. In conclusion, ladies and gentlemen of the jury, I would like to express my sincere regret. I didn't mean for your waste particles to come bubbling up out of the toilet like the Bellagio Fountains in Las Vegas. I can only hope that some of you were playing "God Bless America" during the eruption, as it would have made it more fun. Really, people, I was only trying to help a friend (yes, she was a girl, fine, okay?) by watching her apartment while she was away, not cause Kitty Litter Armageddon..

Ahem . . . back to the point at hand. A friend, an audience, or even an condo association all have one thing in common—their emotions are like a dimmer switch. They can and do oscillate drastically during a show and even an emergency evacuation. In the case of the former, if a comedian is funny and engaging, the switch gets turned up. If, however, a comedian doesn't pull their weight and is not funny, or blasts diarrhea particles into the atmosphere, the dimmer switch gets turned down. Consequently, the room gets quiet, the vibe goes flat, and, along with it, so does *everyone's* act, including mine.

Having realized this over time, I changed my approach completely. Whereas before I only wanted the audience to positively respond to *my* act, now I do everything I can to turn the dimmer as high as it can go for *every performer* and thus keep the flow going. For example, instead of sitting in the back of the room and pouting when a comedian got a laugh, now I sit as close to the stage as I can and I laugh myself silly at every comedian that comes on stage. They've all got some funny to share; otherwise, they wouldn't be up there. Sometimes it's brilliant and hysterical, and admittedly, sometimes it's a train wreck. But even when it is a train wreck, you can still find the funny and have a great time watching them. If the Bellagio Kitty Litter Shit Box Fountain can entertain and create a little joy in this world, so can any and every comedian, even Judy.

What happens when I do this? Very insightful question 8.5" × 11," can I call you "Letter"? Because I'm laughing, each comedian gets at least some positive feedback. Thus, they are more confident on stage. They slow down. They *feel* their humor. They are present. The audience is in sync and connected. They feel the funny too. In short order, the entire crowd warms up. In fact, I've actually experienced myself being the comedian's conduit, connecting them to the audience during their act. Admittedly sometimes it is a bit weird when the comedian realizes that I'm the one person in the crowd responding and starts to perform for just me. I call this the "comedian lap dance"—awk-ward…okay bye, bye..

Most of the time, however, the comedian talks to the broader crowd, and the audience gradually catches on as more people start to respond. By the time my name is called, the audience is warm and so am I. And not just 'cause I've been hanging out in the kiddie pool. I get a great welcome and the people are ready to laugh because they've already been laughing. More and more, I even find myself referring to some of the material the previous comedians shared on stage. This "callback" to their act is an immediate hit because it's already been established as funny with the audience. Again, the preceding comedians being successful on stage sets me up for success. It's just like Newton's law of inertia—an object at rest stays at rest, and an object in motion stays in motion. Likewise, an audience at rest stays at rest, and a laughing audience stays laughing unless acted upon by an unbalanced force, like my grandpa's flatulence or Chewbacca.

In addition to being more enjoyable, creating and supporting the bigger show is so much cooler to do. I'm no longer secretly angry at Harold, thinking his act made mine look like a lazy pile of shame. I love the comedians and they love me back. I support their acts and they do the same for mine. So now, regardless of the audience turnout, I have "friendlies" in the audience, and that's a powerful confidence booster. And, what's more, I have relationships where we are truly happy for each other's success.

Comediology

Mountain View, California. The successful Fortune 500 company where I worked had just been acquired by yet another successful Fortune 500 Company. As a first order of business, both companies had to integrate their respective computer systems so that they could run the operation and

Comediology

report the earnings as "one company." And although it seems simple, this is where the wheels fell off the wagon.

For starters, the acquiring company wanted to do it "their way." After all, *they* were the acquiring company. In the opening scene of the movie *Gladiator*, the decapitated head of a Roman soldier is catapulted toward the invading Roman army. The head lands with a thud and rolls to a stop at a general's feet. The general looks at it and, annoyed, responds, "People should know when they're conquered." I think this is exactly how they saw their acquisition.

The acquired company, on the other hand, did not see things that way at all. After all, they had a far better reputation as it pertained to managerial competence, especially in their Information Technology department. And they'd be damned if the "other side," with all their haphazard shenanigans, was going to take control of this integration. They knew their job and no one was going to tell them how to do it.

I'm sure by now you realize this does not lead to a fairy tale ending. If that's not abundantly obvious to you, well then, honestly, you should read more fairy tales. The analogy was clear in my mind. Both companies boarded the same boat. The boat was launched at full speed and, if not maneuvered correctly, would head directly for a cliff. One side of the boat wanted to go left. The other side wanted to go right. While endless debates were held, neither side would let the other take control of the steering wheel. Because, of course, each was the "rightful and chosen boat captain." (I like that. I think I'm going to make it into a T-shirt. Then I'll give it to two people on the same boat propelling at full speed.)

As this went on, each team felt completely confident in the fact that they were the "right" leadership team. They were convinced that both their leadership and customers would recognize the incompetence of the other team and therefore be completely empowered to lead.

But here's the thing. The customers didn't care who was "right"—they just wanted their services to be enabled. Likewise, the leadership didn't care who was "right" either. They just wanted an end to the escalations from the customers who were no longer getting the great service they had received in the past.

The ironic thing is, there are so many tasks to be done when integrating two companies. You need to combine policies, pricing, products, buildings,

87

customers, marketing campaigns, and the list goes on and on. But these two teams couldn't see it. *They were too caught up in the competition of it.* As a result, they were convinced that there were a limited number of roles. Whenever you feel that the walls are closing in and that there are a limited number of roles or opportunities, there are usually two causes. One, you are dwelling in the competitive world, not the creative one. Or, two, and far less common, you are desperately trapped in the Death Star's trash compactor. Be sure to take a selfie with Chewbacca.

Both teams were sure that they were the superior and rightful owner for this one single effort of many. Consequently, they couldn't step back and think about the fact that perhaps they might find something else that they could perform even better, that might even bring them significantly more fulfillment and joy. They didn't think about what they, themselves, as unique, specially gifted and talented individuals, could bring to an overwhelming situation in dire need of their talents. They just *had* to win the competition and be in control of *this* thing and *these* people.

They were also angry on a day-to-day basis. They told everyone their tale of how righteous they were and how they were being victimized by the other team. They talked about how miserable their lives were because their entitlement was being stripped. If only they could have switched to a creative mindset. If only they could have acknowledged, supported, and perhaps even enjoyed their peer's performances versus fearing and evaluating them, they would have experienced joy and fulfillment versus anger, jealousy, and bitterness and thus expanded their Amway line, to boot.

It was just like the story of the Zax by Dr. Seuss. The North-Going Zax runs into the South-Going Zax on his journey north. Neither Zax will yield and "lower" themselves to step east or west, and so they just stubbornly stand there in each other's way, while all around them an entire city is built.

Yes, an entire city is built around them. In a Dr. Seuss book, where ample real estate and more time are as plentiful as writing another melodic line, having a city built around you while you stubbornly stand still *can* happen. But this is the real world where progress must be demonstrated. And the case of the merger is no exception. So what was the result? *Both* leadership teams got swiftly kicked in the Zaxticals. They were

Comediology

all—yes, *all*—fired. A new leadership team was brought in to integrate the environments. And while each team may have been "right," they certainly weren't getting paid anymore.

If just one side could have acknowledged that perhaps there was value in *something* the other side was doing, it would have been different. If only they could have looked at it as an opportunity to collaborate and create versus compete, the story would have ended differently. Likewise, if my neighbor with the dingleberries had just worked with me, I wouldn't have had to structure my fence so that it blocked out his access to the sun. How are you measuring success in your career? Is it based on your unique gifts and talents in a world of creation? Or, alternatively, is it based on competition? I can't help but think of the movie *There's Something about Mary*. There's a scene where a hitchhiker is explaining his business idea to Ned, the main character, played by Ben Stiller. He asks, "You ever heard of Eight-Minute Abs? Well, we're going to make *Seven*-Minute Abs. And if you aren't satisfied, we'll throw the next minute in for free." Yes, I am taking an example from a fictitious Farrelly Brothers character who just happens to be a serial killer but nevertheless, this is representative. The question is, are *you* tapping into what you do best? Creating it? Or, are you simply making Seven-Minute Abs?

How about your business peers? Are you threatened by them and vice versa because they're on the verge of making Six-Minute Abs while you're trying to anticipate their moves and show up with 5:58-Minute Abs? Are you throwing one another under the bus? How does that make you feel every day? Guarded, bitter, paranoid? How do you think that looks to others in the company or, worse yet, your customers? And what about them? Do you think they're sitting idle while you get the credit for 5:58-Abs? Of course not! They're working on something great, something fantastic, something new and improved—5:57:56 Abs. As you can see, the ab-war cycle continues.

As I've found in comedy, if I tap into and support my colleagues' creativity and uniqueness, I'm not only building a positive relationship based on mutual respect and trust but also building a very robust team with amazing talent. We're not a bunch of five-year-old's playing soccer, all simultaneously chasing the ball around the field. We each play our relevant, unique and respective position. And we do it well because it fits with our gifts and talents.

But wait a second, you say—we're all on the "ab crazy train." Everyone is now building Four-Minute Abs. This is what the culture expects. How do I break this cycle? Well, in my experience, you can't "break" anything. And, from what I've seen, approaching it this way will only get you a $0 bonus and a pile of bad reviews.

It's more apparent when you think about it from a comedian context. If I were to tell my comedian peers, "Hey, when I'm up on stage, you must laugh and support me!" they would most assuredly do just the opposite— heckling the bejesus out of me as I painfully delivered my set. And I mean really, who says stuff like that *besides* Kim Jong-un?

No, to start the cycle of change in comedy, *I* had to be the one to start being supportive. *I* had to be the one to initiate—selflessly listening to their creations and sincerely appreciating their unique comedic offerings. After consistently applying this method over time (yes, it may take more than one night—what do you think we're making here, a baby?!) the most magical thing occurs. The comedians whom I had deeply feared and criticized, reciprocated! I never even had to start the bus, much less throw people under it!

Likewise, in corporate America, *you* must initiate. *You* must be the catalyst for change. *You* must exit the land of competition and inhabit the land of creativity. Do you like building Four-Minute Abs? Not really? Okay, then, what *do* you like? What interests *you*? Start there. What fits with *your* unique skillset and passion? What can *you* create? Can you write the letters "Y-O-U" in *italics?* No? Good, then leave that bit to me, I'm super good at it. Maybe you can add the period, though

Note: This will take time to build, but keep at it. Follow this line of thinking. It is a process. And unless you're an overnight sensation, or Justin Bieber, it will take time. Regardless of the time it takes, it will snatch you from the world of competition and place you smack dab in the world of creativity, which is a *much* more fun, supportive, and fulfilling place to live.

"But I don't know what I want to be when I grow up!" Yes, I too recall the illusory need to have my destination of who and what I would be etched in stone. I would claim that destination to myself and my friends: an accountant, an actor, an executive, a stand-up comedian, and so on. Then, after some

Comediology

time, the path deviated as paths tend to do. Thus, I felt like a phony, a fraud, someone who just couldn't make up their mind and stick to the path.

Now however, I realize that we've all missed the plot! Life's isn't about a destination, a "what." How boring would that be? Life, I think, is purposely designed to let you experience variety with different people, different situations, and different roles. None of this would be possible if you picked just one role for the rest of your life. So, for starters, I would suggest just making the conscious choice to live in the land of creativity and go where the path takes you. No destination. No press announcements. No pressure. Just enjoy the ride and have fun.

I remember when I was initially dipping my toe into the world of creativity. One of the things that helped me get clear on my path was something I learned from my former boss and, to this day, mentor. I confided in her and told her how unfulfilled I felt in doing what I was doing. At the time, I was essentially making 3:56 Abs and developing a roadmap to deliver 3:55 Abs shortly thereafter.

She asked me to simply write down three things that I wanted to do and, along with those, three things I did *not* want to do—a very simple formula. It did not contain the key ingredient that I thought I needed—a tangible destination. Over time, however, I realized it was much more helpful and meaningful than that. It got me in touch with my preferences and predilections. After working so many years in corporate America, this was something I'd forgotten to do. I know, it sounds crazy but it's true. There's only so many times you can suggest a creative idea and have it detonate into a public mushroom-cloud camel fart, that you start to think, "Hmmm . . . no you're right Melissa, everyone just loves being under constant surveillance."

I've learned that this formula can and should be used iteratively. Once I learn more about the path I'm on, I can always go back to my list of three do's and three don'ts and alter the path accordingly.

Continual creativity is now something that fulfills me and makes me more effective, whether I'm crafting something on my own or working in a team. I always knew I enjoyed being creative, but I never thought about it as a door to more opportunities. But when you stop and think about it, we're always looking for faster, better, and cheaper. As this occurs, industries become commoditized, and lower-cost or more efficient methods will replace higher-cost or less efficient ones. To see evidence of this, we need look no further than our past.

In 1930, 41 percent of the United States was working in agriculture; now it's less than 2 percent. In 1950, 34 percent was working in manufacturing; now it's less than 13 percent. The economy is relentless at continually repeating this pattern. This is great news for us consumers because it provides goods and services that are faster, better, and cheaper. But what if we're not the consumer, but the supplier? Everything is constantly changing and it seems there is no safe place! What's stopping my organization or job from ultimately becoming a commodity or, worse yet, a line of code?

Here's the great news. The catalyst for change that we all fear is actually the one thing the economy cannot commoditize; on the contrary, it's actually dependent upon it to grow! The catalyst for change is that original idea or invention. It is that spark of ingenuity that gets us to try something we wouldn't have otherwise. It is that bold, new, and different process or product that no one has ever thought of before. And, of course, it always starts with one thing—creativity.

Your creativity is limited only by your imagination. It's original and it's yours. You can't automate, right-size, outsource, or offshore it. How could you? Whether you work in an organization or department, or as an individual, take the time to invest in, articulate, and pursue your creativity. It's the one thing that will always keep you from becoming a commodity.

As you exert your creativity, you'll feel more fulfilled—after all, you are creating something special and unique that is based upon you and your unique talents. You'll find that you are more supportive of others and them of you because you start to recognize and give them credit for their unique talents and gifts. This enables all of you to bring unique value to the table and create something neither of you could do by yourself or by copying one other.

In addition to being a fulfilling experience for you, this transition will be immensely valuable to your customers. Instead of a cutthroat competition for the best individual performer temporarily clutching the winning copycat formula, you are now showing up as a team of uniquely talented individuals. Your colleagues have "warmed up the stage" for you, and you for them.

Comediology

Both the Zen philosophy and Nike founder Phil Knight's book *Shoe Dog* tell us that the self is merely an illusion, and when it comes to competition, we can only be victorious when we forget the self and the opponent. After all, they are but two parts of the same whole. I have found this to be true in comedy, where competing is limiting and otherwise detrimental to the bigger show. It also rings true in business where competition will rapidly turn you into a bitter commodity. The path, *the true path*, therefore, is to turn inward and embrace your unique gift of creativity. Once you do, you will differentiate yourself. You will enjoy. And you will find that, yes, you still have a young, vibrant soul (unless you unwittingly traded it for some mesquite-flavored pork skins). This, by the way, is the true fountain of youth and is much more effective than any diet or skin cream. Which of course is the real point of this entire book. If a person is funny, no one will notice they have dry, flaky skin and are not on a diet.

Summary

Living in the world of competition, looking outside of yourself for ideas and inspiration, limits your goals as well as your potential. So dig deep and embrace from within:

1) **Exit the world of competition; live in the world of creation.** Start from what your heart and soul are telling you and work outward from there, not the other way around.

2) **Embrace your unique gift of creativity.** Let go of judgment, especially on yourself, and follow your creativity to where it leads you. If you truly can let go, it will be a gloriously fun adventure.

3) **Find where you uniquely fit and play.** Einstein never made the cut to be quarterback for the Denver Broncos; thank goodness he embraced his distinctiveness.

4) **Tap into and support your colleagues' creativity and uniqueness. You will build not only positive relationships based on mutual respect and trust, but also a very robust team with amazing talent.** Your colleagues are a group of individuals, each with their own unique talents and aspirations. Don't force them into a box; instead, encourage them to get out of theirs.

5) **You must be the catalyst for change.** Don't expect the culture to shift on a dime. Encourage yourself and others to embrace their gifts. Keep at it and, over time, you'll see the results.

6) **Write down three things that you want to do and, along with those, three things you do not want to do.** This will open the door and help you figure out your hidden inspiration.

Everything is funny, as long as it's happening to someone else.

—*Will Rogers*

Vulnerability

I knew the oldest beginner comedian ever. His name was Remmy. He was just learning comedy at eighty-five years old. It was amazing, and I secretly wondered if his next stop would be rugby.

It was obvious he was timeworn. When he walked—or, more accurately, hobbled—to the stage, he did so slowly. He looked feeble, as if he should be attached to an intravenous feeding tube with someone permanently accompanying him who was constantly verbalizing encouraging, yet slightly condescending, accolades like, "Nice job, Remmy, you're going to break the track record here at Al's Seafood Restaurant."

Remmy finally made it to the stage and grabbed the microphone. He held it for a moment. While he did get the audience's attention, you couldn't help but feel sorry for Remmy. You were certain that at any given moment, he would collapse and it would be all over.

As he contemplated what he was going to say into the microphone, silence engulfed the scene. You could hear a cricket scratch his inner thigh. We wanted—no, we *needed* to listen attentively. We had to show Remmy that we cared about what he was saying to avoid hurting his feelings or showing any sign of disrespect. After all, *we* didn't want to be the one who caused the kidney failure.

Then Remmy began. Like gravel churning in a cement mixer, Remmy's voice was gruff and raspy. Surely his larynx had been used to load coal for several decades by now. Slowly, and in a faint Bostonian accent, he painstakingly delivered his first line. "I've just recovered from a stroke," he claimed. *Oh. Wow*, we thought. If we didn't feel bad enough for Remmy to begin with, this undoubtedly put us over the edge. Way over the edge. I felt excruciatingly guilty for not having to wear dentures and diapers.

He continued. "The doctor says I now have a heightened case of disinhibition." We audience members were dumbstruck. Was this a comedy act or some type of charity "bucket list" event for senior citizens

Chris S. Tabish with Kurtis Matthews

on hospice row? Was he going to ask for money, or worse, hand out bingo cards? Was Sally Struthers up next? Instead of a rowdy comedy club, the ambience had been reduced to an awkwardly reverent funeral—"I never knew Remmy but, goddammit, he was a good man!"

What was going on? Nobody actually knew what the hell "disinhibition" was, but it sure didn't sound good." I was trying to think of other diseases that started with "dis" but couldn't come up with any. Well, almost. I did suffer an affliction from the "dis" family in junior high school. It flared up whenever I tried to impress the opposite sex. I think they called it "disappointing." It was apparently a very severe case.

Remmy paused for sympathetic effect. This was about as necessary as voice mail instructions. ("At the sound of the beeping tone, just leave me your information including your name and your phone number—oh, and if you want to send me a fax. . . ." Seriously, people, are we not yet be done with the faxes?) He looked solemnly out at the audience as if to say, "For crying out loud people, I need help here."

After a long and extremely uncomfortable silence, it looked like he would finally continue. Or drop dead. We weren't quite sure. Oh, God, what was next? Did he suffer from irritable bowel syndrome, too? Did his pet hamster have leukemia? Was he pregnant? I'm not sure I could take anymore. We all sat in our chairs unable to breathe, much less move.

Thank goodness, Remmy finally broke the silence. "Yes, that's right, 'disinhibition,' which basically means, I don't give a fuck."

Hearing this, the audience roared with laughter. In a single punch line, Remmy spontaneously transformed from Gollum to Jimmy Fallon. Our perception of him was completely changed. We were no longer feeling sorry *for* him; we were completely *with* him. He was no longer that weirdly muted uncle we placated with a perfunctory smile on our way to the potato salad. No, not at all. He was now part of the in crowd. He was one of us. We *adored* him. We were in awe of him. And we couldn't wait to hear what he was going to say next. It was one of the most amazing openers I've ever witnessed.

To Prove or To Be? That Is The Question

On stage, the initial funny that comes out of your mouth is, no surprise, your "opener." Just like meeting someone for the first time, you

Comediology

have seconds to make that first impression. Do you want to befriend? Shock? Make them believe? Or question? Regardless of your approach, one thing is for sure: they will be watching. And whether you, or they, are even aware of it, they will be assessing and judging you. Like droplets of water, their hidden biases and prejudices gradually condense, accumulate, and soon form into an impression of you. And that's it. You're either on the right side of the fence, or you're not. You're either in or you're out. But rest assured, it happens. Because that's how we're wired.

When I started out, my opener was formed out of fear. In other words, I felt that if I didn't come out strong and "prove" my comedic worthiness with some serious laughter, I would be found a fake, a phony. This far outweighed my intention of making any audience connection or having fun. My approach was something like this. . . .

"Oh, wow, look at this audience we have here tonight! You know how sometimes, you can tell just by looking at people that they're amazing and they're going to be a spectacular audience?

"Yeah, well, it's too bad you're not those kind of people."

After shamelessly performing this opener several times, Martin Shervington, a fellow comedian and friend whose opinion I respect, came up to me and gave me some feedback: "Chris, the opener gets a chuckle, sure, but you're alienating your audience. Right out of the gate you're offending them. Then, if you do that, you have to win them back and it's an uphill battle. Why not start out easier and get them on your side first?"

I thought about what he told me. Yes, I was offending my audience, but isn't that what comedians did? Like *all* of the time?! I know *I've* been called out when I was naïve enough to sit in the front row with a first date. Isn't that how it was done? Now I wasn't so sure. After all, upon reflection, and so many years later, that comedian was a real bastard. And not just according to me. Just ask the girl I never saw again because he convinced the crowd we looked too much like "cousins" to be seriously dating. Surely, we had mixed up "first date" with "family reunion." It probably didn't help matters that we were in Utah at the time.

I searched for the answer with my fellow comedians. I asked audience members. I even tried accessing the "Omniscient Guide to What People Are Thinking about You" which apparently hasn't been written yet. With all kinds of input swirling in my head, I decided to do my own "opener" experiment.

I liked the basic premise of my old opener. I thought it had a good setup and I also liked the "reveal" or punch line. That said, I wanted to change the point of view. I had to rewrite it in a way where I wasn't immediately offending my audience. I even went further to make it self-deprecating. Here's what I came up with. . . .

"I was nervous about getting on stage tonight. I asked the host what he thought. He said, 'Don't worry about it. You know how you see someone and you can just tell by the way they walk and the way they talk that they're going to move an audience?'"

"I replied knowingly and said, 'Oh yeah, ha, ha, I know what you mean.'"

"And then he said, 'Yeah, well, that guy cancelled about an hour ago, so get your butt up on stage.'"

The audience reaction from the rewrite was night-and-day different from the original. People laughed uninhibited. The interesting thing was it was the same basic joke! The only modification was that it was told from a different perspective. In other words, I was throwing *myself* under the bus.

So, what really made the difference? To answer it, I think it's helpful to walk through the mindsets of the different parties involved—otherwise known as me and the audience.

To start, here's what *I* was thinking telling the original joke:

"Oh, there's my name being called. I'm up to bat. Oh, %@#$! I'd better throw down some comedy chops quick or they're going to realize I didn't learn comedy at Harvard. This joke's funny and, even more, it's biting. No one will want to mess with me after I tell it. Mmwaaahaaahaaaa! And while you're at it, I'll have [pinky pose] *one million dollars*! And yes, *of course* they'll see I'm just kidding."

What *they*, the audience, were (probably) thinking with the original joke:

"Hmmm . . . wouldn't mind another beer. Wait, who's on stage? Oh, someone new. Hey, where's my beer? Hey . . . what?! Was that joke aimed at me? OK, I'd better get my defenses up. I don't want to stand out in this crowd in front of this guy. I really need another beer."

Here's what *I* was thinking with the *rewrite*:

100

Comediology

"Oh, there's my name being called. I'm up to bat. Okay, I'd better throw down some comedy chops quick. I know, I'll let them see my ridiculous ego. That's funny, even to me! Yes, it's embarrassing, too, but only for me, and since laughing with others outweighs my need to be Rico Suave (feel free to look it up), I don't care, why should anyone else? Let's roll!"

What the audience was (probably) thinking with the rewrite:

"Hmmm . . . wouldn't mind another beer. Wait, who's on stage? Oh, someone new. Oh, man, that guy's ego—what a slam! I'll bet he felt like a total jackass. I've felt that way before. I can totally relate. That's funny. What's he going to say next?"

No matter what kind of bad day you think you're having or how nervous you feel on stage, chances are people aren't seeing that. Believe it or not, people are only seeing the "good" side of being you. In fact, they might even be seeing you in one of your most confident moments. After all, you're on stage, where you have the audacity to perform in front of all those people. Even if you bomb, it still takes confidence. And, at the very least, the audience will see and respect that. As Lucille Ball stated, "I'm not funny. What I am is brave." Therefore, when you come at them from a "I'm gonna poke you in the eye, loser; no, just kidding" perspective, it goes over like a Trump tweet in Hollywood.

You know how when you're getting dressed in the morning and you're thinking you want people to see the best side of you—attractive, in shape, confident, and so forth? We want people to see this within us because we want to be noticed. We want to be appreciated. We want to be accepted and we want to be loved. Well, guess what? They *do* see it. That's the good news. But, funny enough, looking good doesn't necessarily bring us the results we want. Just ask any model, reality TV star, or Ann Coulter. In fact, it can have the reverse effect, especially if we're poking fun at them. And yes, even if it's just to cover up our own insecurities.

To put it in diametrically contrasting terms on a narrowly defined spectrum, we are either an "underdog" or a "jackass." We've all played both parts and have been perceived as each. So, what's the difference? For starters, jackasses by nature are insensitive, or at least come across that way. They often poke but do not reveal. They find humor in others' insecurities but are stone-faced when it comes to their own. Their egos are fragile

101

Chris S. Tabish with Kurtis Matthews

and their tempers are short. They embrace "normal" and "standard," and anything that is different or exceptional, they shun, disregard, or outright annihilate. They are constantly trying to prove the rightness of their world, yet, ironically, live in fear that they too will be ultimately be revealed as a freak. Therefore, they find fault in others and repress, or desperately hide, the freak within themselves. Because of this, they secretly and fiercely have sensual and musky man envy for the underdogs.

Completely opposite of the jackasses are the underdogs. They accept and embrace their freak flags. They have little to no ego. In fact, they might even call attention to their "shortcomings." This self-deprecation shows their vulnerability. This vulnerability makes them shine with an inner glow that can't be emulated by the jackass's veneer of bravado.

The underdog gives others a picture of what it's like being inside the mind of an imperfect human being. They are not victims. That said, they have no problem letting people know of their struggles and how they feel about them. Their challenges are daunting, but you can identify with them. *This* is why they are underdogs. And what do we do with underdogs? We cheer for them. We want them to win!

Jackasses, of course, are often the favorites to win. On the outside, we see an arrogant demeanor and very little that can challenge them. And what do we want for the jackasses? We want them to *lose*! Or more accurately, we want them to get beat by the underdog.

Underdogs demonstrate the humanity within all of us. You get that they regularly experience the gamut of emotions—excitement, fear, joy, and insecurity—*just like everyone else on the planet*. They're not trying to *prove* anything. They are simply *being themselves*. Through this humility and openness, they enable commonality with other people. In fact, people adore them because they provide a shared experience and a perfect platform to create a positive and fun exchange. They let their freak flags fly. As a result, they evade all judgment, and what remains is understanding, empathy, and, yes, funny.

Comediology

How many times have you started a job or joined a team or led a presentation thinking, "I've got to *prove myself*?" I certainly have. It's easy to fall into this trap. But from my experience, it's counterintuitive and can

Comediology

be a serious setback. Being vulnerable and letting people see the human side of you pays off *way* more than setting out to "prove" yourself. Besides, what are you—a math equation? You really do exist without the validation of other people's opinions and a dirty protractor. I promise.

It is important to point out a critical distinction. Focusing on your craft and delivering quality in whatever it is that you do is a must. As human and vulnerable as it might be, nobody wants an extra serving of "useless," "helpless victim," or stale zebra balls.

So, yes, you need to perform and you need to do it well. But you can't do it in a vacuum. And you certainly can't do it at the expense of building a relationship with others. After all, what company, team, or idea doesn't need people rallying behind it to make it successful? And who are those people going to support—the jackass or the underdog?

When you are vulnerable and let people in to see the real you, in addition to performing your role, people "get" you. They relate to you. They find things in you that are in common with themselves and therefore can see your side of the story. As such, they will want to support you and help you be successful.

In addition to the prestigious research I've done at the renowned Purple Onion Comedy Club, there is apparently "other" research that supports this phenomenon as well. For example, Tiziana Casciaro and Miguel Sousa Lobo conclude in their *Harvard Business Review* article, "Competent Jerks, Lovable Fools, and the Formation of Social Networks," that how a person feels about you plays a more critical role than their evaluation of your competence.

According to the study, a person may be competent, but if they're disliked, people still don't want to work with them—shocker! Conversely, if someone *is* liked, their colleagues will do all that they can to tap into all the competence that person can offer. "We're gonna find that gold, matey, wherever it may be!" This tendency is not just in corner cases but is generally applicable.

People will see your competence. Or they won't. It's either there, or it isn't. Either way, you don't need to *prove* anything. It is what it is. The matter of competence, however, pales in the comparison to the more important question: Who are *you*? From another's perspective, are you a person that is humble? Do you have self-awareness? Can you laugh at

103

Chris S. Tabish with Kurtis Matthews

yourself? Can you acknowledge your mistakes? Can I relate to you? Could I work with you? Can I trust you? And perhaps, most importantly, can I borrow your cat?

These questions cannot be answered by a left-brained, analytical presentation. And, from my experience, if they aren't answered and people don't know who you are, they often don't assume the best. Put simply and dichotomously, if your presentation demonstrates competence without vulnerability, in their eyes you just might be a threat, a menace—yes, a jackass.

Therefore, and right off the bat, let people in to experience the *human* side of you. Understand that they will naturally see your competence and so let the rest of you be known. Push beyond your comfort zone to get out there. Tell a personal story about yourself, make a self-deprecating comment, or tell them about a relevant, amusing mistake you once made. I strongly recommend that funny be your ally during this, as it helps tap into their emotions, versus their analytical minds, and you will connect more effectively.

Let them know you don't take yourself that seriously and that you are human just like they are, and watch what happens. My experience at work is the same one I've had on stage. If you let people in to see the real you, it builds a strong foundation based on authenticity, empathy, and trust, and they will support you in any way they can.

Every time I reflect on this subject, I can't help think about Superman. Here's a hero with super powers way beyond what you or I will ever experience; well yeah, I mean *outside* of my math-class fantasies.

Superman saved numerous people and prevented countless crimes. That said, in many plotlines, we see the crowd turning on him. He's Superman, people! What the hell is going on?! Well, put simply, we the audience see everything—his heroics, his struggles, and, most importantly, his vulnerability. But everyone else who lives in Metropolis only sees a glimpse of this, and then make up their own story. Where was Superman when my toe was stepped on at the fair?! Where was Superman when we ran out of dishwashing detergent at the Christmas event?! Where was *"Superman"* when I decided to drop thousands of dollars in merchandise and blame it on Beence?! Where was *"Superman"* for the past eight months

Comediology

when Clark Kent went missing? Hey, wait a darn minute! Were those two dating?

Here's the takeaway. And yes, it's a ridiculous for a reason—you'll remember it. If Superman, in a fabricated world, using all his super powers, can't maintain a constant, positive perception from everyone at all times, then we don't have a snowball's chance in hell of doing so. Therefore, don't try it. At least, don't try it by using your super powers. Just be *you*— vulnerable, human, fallible, and, yes, even funny.

Summary

To be or not to be . . . a jackass or underdog? That is the question. In other words, who do people experience when they interact with you? Is it an authentic human who is flawed, vulnerable, and therefore likeable and human? Or is it Biff from *Back to the Future*? Remember, people don't see our insecurities like we think they do. In fact, they often perceive a better side of you than you give yourself credit for. If you don't show them the human side early and often, they will make up their own story, and that's usually not a good thing. Other tips that will help include:

1) **Let go of your need to prove yourself.** I mean, let's be real, did this ever work out for you in Geometry 101? What makes you think it will be any better dealing with people?

2) **If you demonstrate competence without vulnerability, in their eyes you just might be a threat, a menace—yes, a jackass.** Therefore, let people in to experience the human side of you in addition to the competent side of you. In other words, let them into your heart as well as your head.

3) **Push beyond your comfort zone to make a connection.** Tell a personal story about yourself, make a self-deprecating comment, or tell them about a relevant, amusing mistake you made. I strongly recommend that funny be your ally during this, as it helps tap into their emotions, versus their analytical minds, and you will connect more effectively.

4) **Let people in to see the real you.** This will build a strong foundation based on authenticity, empathy, and trust, and the people you let in will support you in any way they can.

If someone ever tells you that you're putting too much peanut butter on, stop talking to them. You don't need that negativity in your life.

—Anonymous

Feedback. It's Not about You. No, Really Though.

I love the movies. Some of my favorite movies portray characters that are absolute freak-show train wrecks. Take for example the movie *Goodfellas*. In this movie, there is this character named Tommy DeVito played by Joe Pesci. Tommy is sort of like the Enron of human beings. He lies, cheats, robs, smacks, slaps, shoots, kills, and has a Napoleon complex.

He shot a gofer in the foot for not being quick with his drink, only to kill him later when he dared to be sassy to him (oh and no, not that kind of gofer! That kind of gopher is spelled with a "ph" and besides, they don't have feet! Seriously, come on people? OK, yes it's true, I had to look it up myself and no, as it turns out, you can't in fact shoot a gopher, just ask Bill Murray). He beat up a restaurant owner who asked him to settle his exceedingly large and overdue tab. And, oh yeah, he stuck an icepick into the skull of one of his closest associates and he wasn't even frozen at the time.

He does, however, love his mother. Sure, he lies to her, but loves her just the same. Put simply, he's like Hitler without all the charisma and vegetarianism.

In spite of all of this, I still paid good money to see him. And a lot of others just like him. Why? Because, well, simply put, he's not "normal." He's a total freak show! And it's fascinating to watch someone like this. How could anyone act this way, much less be a depiction of a real person? And, yes, Mom definitely exposed me to many chemicals in my childhood. It was probably the fabric softener, the fried bologna with ketchup, or the nonstop flow of cigarette smoke from Uncle Ernie, aka "the bald dragon."

That said, I know I'm not alone. Many people *loved* this movie and a lot of others with crazy freak shows. From Darth Vader in *Star Wars*, to Biff Tannen in *Back To The Future*, to anyone with a bad Russian accent in a Liam Neeson movie, we love watching those freak flags fly! The freakier, the more delicious. Here's my twelve dollars for the movie AMC, thank you! Oh, right, and the twenty-six dollars for the popcorn. No, I don't want to supersize it for another fifty cents. But thanks for that awkward inquiry that makes me look cheap and financially incompetent in front of a crowd— 'preciate ya.

When you walk out of the theater and return to real life, those freaks should remain in the digital format from which they came. But somehow, like those pesky garden gnomes that travel to Europe with seemingly no moving body parts, they sneak out and you actually see them in real life. And they cause every kind of drama and stress imaginable. They don't listen, they offend, they're insensitive, arrogant, or destroy the elevator ambience by wearing too much grandma perfume that smells like sugar cookies and bad Christmas gifts.

I used to get so upset when dealing with a freak in real life. I would mull the interactions over and over in my mind and get completely stressed out. Why are they acting that way? Did I cause this? Don't they like me? How should I deal with this? Do I need to change? My diaper? Just checking to see if you were still paying attention.

Do I try and approach them? Do I try and gain allies? Do I act nonchalant? Or should I flash them some wicked stank eye that I learned back in prison? Well, okay, it's true, I've never been arrested. However, I did watch every season of *Orange Is the New Black,* so I'm totally hip to the scene.

I spent so much time in my head with this useless mind chatter. It wasn't until much later in life that I learned the simple truth. I learned that those freak-show train wrecks have nothing to do with me. Yes, that's right. A freak-show train wreck is a freak-show train-wreck, regardless of me or my actions. Period.

Have you ever tried to change one of these people? Oh, and bonus question, did it work? You can't change these people because *it isn't about you.* It's quite simple, really. If it *were* about you, maybe you could change them, but it's not, so, well, you can't.

If only they'd have taught this basic associative property in school, I would have saved countless hours on anxiety-ridden self-talk comingled with fantasies of vengeance. Yes, I think you know what I'm talking about.

Comediology

We all have them and they all start out the same. A long time ago in a galaxy far, far away—or, put another way, about forty-two minutes ago in the corporate boardroom—our "hero" has been "wronged' in his righteous quest for glory. (Yes, "hero," that's me. What do you keep looking at?!). We join our hero live at the scene. . . .

I've had it up to here. I am committed to taking a stand not only for me but the countless, innocent others who also have been persecuted, demoralized, or otherwise ignored. You know, like Gina from Accounts Payable. I courageously go to the battlefield where bloody confrontations and savage beatings occur every day—the conference room on the fourth floor, just past the coffee machine. With determined force, I summon the key that will allow me entry into the arena. With bulging forearm muscles, I yank down on the retractable clasp attached to my belt loop and steady my security badge against the pad until the indicator light turns green. Upon seeing this, I wildly thrust open the doors like John Wayne in a new town, or for you Millennials out there, Rango. Everyone turns their gaze to me in stunning amazement at both my bravery and perfectly jelled hair with just the right amount of puddin'.

I see my assailant standing in front of the room. I see also that he is armed. With a look of scorn, he thrusts his weapon toward the PowerPoint being displayed on the screen. "As you can see, Chris's department is lagging by 32 percent!"

I call on the words that I know will enforce peace and justice, if only for the moment. "I don't think we're singing from the same hymn sheet!" I cry out. "We need to drill down and peel this onion—full stop."

He stops in mid-stride as if suspended in quicksand. The meeting attendees realize that this is no ordinary meeting and exchange glances of mounting anticipation.

I then tell the freak-show train wreck everything that everyone has been thinking about telling him but has been too fearful to say—"You never gave out the equity you promised!" I accuse. "You're too afraid to give an employee feedback in a personal conversation so you yell at them in front of the whole company!" I continue. "You have at least six multimillion-dollar properties yet don't pay out bonuses!"

I notice beads of sweat form on his bald head as I go on. "You are a horrible leader and inspire no one! You lack integrity, honesty, and if it were possible, you would trade the Golden Rule in for shares of Webvan! Well, the joke's on you cause that's not even a company anymore! Do you ever wonder why every person you've ever hired has left the company and you have no friends? Here's a hint—you are an absolute and complete jackass! And one more thing—you smell like peanut butter did aerobics in 1981 and never showered after that. I think it's your soul!"

While both he and the audience sit in stunned silence, I quickly shoot him in the forehead with a Nerf plunger dart. I then swiftly launch into an Olympic-style backflip. Jumping several feet into the air, I gracefully twist my body one full revolution and then, ever so stylishly, touch down atop the freshly waxed conference table in a perfect Bruce Lee Dragon Pose. I stare my defeated boss in the eye. My head shakes violently as I furiously let out a high-pitched victory cry—"Whhaaaaaaaaa!"

A broader audience has spontaneously materializes. It's everyone I like or have ever wanted to impress. They are witnessing and relishing this magnificent event. I turn to my assailant and deliver one final blow: "Your performance is unacceptable. As a result, we'll be letting you go in the same manner you have let so many go before you—the day before your vacation." The spectators rise and give a standing ovation. Hoots and hollers of triumph reverberate throughout the kingdom—err, conference room. I bow humbly while a glory horn blows in the distance, loudly signaling the unquestionable victory witnessed by the masses.

It's a beautiful thing to dispose of the freak-show train wreck. But here's the *really* scary part—we've *all* been guilty of being a freak-show train wreck. Okay, maybe not as bad as Moldy Peanut Butter Soul-Cheese Guy, but nevertheless, it's true. One saving grace is that it comes in two flavors. Option one is temporary and a result of you having a #@$-fest of a day. Think of this option not as an on/off switch, but more like a light dimmer. It's usually off until you inadvertently vacuum up my cat's soul.

Option two is apparently as close to "permanent" as anything gets in this lifetime. This is truly unfortunate for them and, more so, everyone else but them.

Sadly, you probably aren't going to witness moldy peanut butter soul guy realizing the error of his ways and changing anytime soon. So let's

Comediology

focus on where there's actual hope. Here's a real-life example of option one, the temporary freak-show train wreck.

My in-laws are some of the greatest people I know. Yes, I seriously won the in-law lottery. They are warm, generous, kind-hearted old souls to the core. That said, many years back in the "old country," aka Oregon, my father-in-law had a heated debate with one of their family friends. Well, let's be real. When I say "heated," I mean a volcanic sacrifice to the gods would be a mere dip in the Frito Lay bean tub compared to this incident. To protect the innocent, we'll call my father-in-law "Bill" and the family friend "Janice." But their real names are Denny and Margie. The topic was benign, and frankly, quite mundane really. Here goes. And please be prepared with a caffeine injection. Trust me, you'll need it.

The topic that made the world stand on end for a day was none other than "frozen berries." You argue interracial marriage, religion, and politics? The *New York Times* gives you five stars, sure. However, the *Idaho Gazette*, in all its glory, would give you only two stars because it simply can't justify it when compared to their fan favorite, frozen berries.

The frozen-berry apocalypse started out quite innocently. Denny was espousing the opinion that, nowadays, berries were frozen with a "flash" technology that was so sudden, so instantaneous, it would literally freeze the berry on impact. Thus, when it was thawed, days, weeks, or months later, it would taste as garden-fresh and delicious as if it were just picked from the vine.

"Nonsense!" refuted Margie. "There is no frozen berry on the planet that would taste the same as a fresh berry regardless of the technological means of freezing it."

Okay, there you have it—quite a mundane dispute, right? If the debate over UFOs is a 9.6 out of 10 on the interesting scale, then I'd give this like a .000002, rounded up to the nearest peso. One might conclude, "Each to their own opinion," "We agree to disagree," and off we go because, let's face it, what's the point of arguing this? I mean, after all, there's plenty to do—reruns of *Matlock* that need watching and so forth.

On that particular day, however, I'm not sure whether people didn't have enough sleep, or the Earth's axis was tilted just enough to materially affect the horoscopic outlook, but *this* was the verbal battle of the decade— "Berry Wars." Seriously, examples were cited, sides were taken, children were sacrificed, and even a dragon was hatched from a once-thought petrified egg and engaged in fiery combat. Everyone involved instantly turned into a freak-show-train-wreck. The roof was on fire and evidently nobody needed water but rather all chose to let that mother@!#!er burn.

And burn it did. It got to such a heated point that, had it not been for the legendary taste of Denny's barbeque or the much-heeded advice you could only get from Margie after being a teacher for umpteen years, I'm not sure the band ever would have gotten back together. It took a lot of time and gallons of honey-mesquite glaze to mend but alas, after many moons, the frozen berry topic had been laid to rest—hopefully permanently, but one never knows. . . .

And to this day, the cautionary tale is told. In fact, I wasn't even there; I read it off some golden scrolls I found buried under the La-Z-Boy. This happened over fifteen years ago but even now, anyone, and I mean ANYONE, who comments on the taste, texture, or quality of a frozen berry as compared to a fresh berry, the walls come alive with a wave-like rippling. Heads turn 180 degrees. And the words "GET OUT" spontaneously appear smudged on the window fog, and it's "instant freak-show train-wreck city" for all.

That's option one. And while it can be severe, it's usually a one-hit wonder. Option two of being a freak-show train wreck is permanent. If you are this type of freak show, you're probably the result of a sperm that, instead of working hard swimming your critical life-lap up the stream, *you* took the journey by riding on the shoulders of a hard-working, more dignified sperm. Then, at the last possible second, you leaped off the hard-working sperm's shoulders while simultaneously shoving him backward. You then landed on the coveted egg . . . first. And that's the way you were conceived. You bastard. No wonder your soul smells like mold.

Regardless of the type of train wreck you are, it is important to recognize that anytime you are interacting with people, while we hope for sunny weather, there will always be the chance of freak-show precipitation. It could happen anytime like a hurricane, earthquake, or wardrobe mishaps during the Super Bowl halftime show. You've got no control over it. This is a very depressing thought until you realize that it's akin to something we all love and adore—the movies. Yes, that's right. Somehow, we're under this illusion that we should be able to control the things in our life, and we

Comediology

really resent it when we can't. Yet in the movies, the more out of control, the better. Remember this the next time you encounter a freak-show train wreck. They'll probably be berating you because you did something like unwittingly put the vacuum hose too close to their cat and sucked out its spirit. And they're absolutely certain of it. Kitty-Mitten has not been the same ever since! That said, don't hop aboard the train to "crazy town" just yet. Remember that it's not about you. Obviously. Also remember that you typically have to pay good money for entertainment like this but you're getting it for *free* ($26 popcorn and a questionably sticky floor not included).

Instead of resenting them, simply enjoy their performance. The more you can take it in as an act, the better off it will be for both of you. You, because you won't go to jail for stuffing a crazy person inside of a vacuum. Them, because they got it out of their system and have "exorcised the daehmons!" And, if they're really fortunate, you've given them some constructive feedback for their next performance. Yeah, perhaps the fiery spray of saliva could spew out as the finale rather than the opener? Just a thought. . . .

As a stand-up comic, you get lots of feedback. This feedback can range from "You're the greatest!" to utter silence to "You're an a**hole, get off the stage." Given the option, I might suggest the former. At first, the negative feedback was hurtful and I took it very personally. Then I realized two very important truths.

First, as in real life, in any audience, there will be a representative sample of freak-show train wrecks. When they flare up, it's not about me. It's about them. They are living in their own world and I'm simply their stimulus.

Second, when I'm on stage, I'm delivering material. My material is not me but is a completely separate entity. Don't get me wrong, I really like my material or I wouldn't bring it to the stage with me. That said, for good, bad, or worse, I'm the delivery driver—that's it. Not to diminish the role, as it is important for me as the delivery driver to understand if I'm delivering filet mignon or dingy, fatty zebra balls. I do get valuable feedback from the audience and, if I want to stay in the game, I need to listen to it and adjust accordingly. But it's important to remember that it is feedback on my *material* and not me as a person.

Chris S. Tabish with Kurtis Matthews

This helps me absorb the feedback and really listen to it while not taking it personally.

To summarize, we don't need to look any further than the famous philosopher "Anonymous" and his, or her, famous words of wisdom : "In your twenties and thirties, you worry about what other people think. In your forties and fifties, you stop worrying about what other people think. And in your sixties and seventies, you realize they were never thinking about you in the first place."

Comediology

As in comedy, in business it's easy to fall into the trap of taking feedback personally. If you've ever had a job but have never encountered a freak-show train-wreck situation, you are either extremely lucky or extremely medicated. Either way, keep doing what you're doing 'cause it's working exceptionally well. For the rest of us, there is good news. You just need to take it in stride. When the interaction gets so crazy that you're sincerely wondering if you did, in fact, vacuum up a cat's soul, then you've lost your grip and need to reset. Again, it's not about you. The person with whom you're interacting has just boarded the crazy train and my advice to you would be not to hop aboard with them.

In freak-show train-wreck scenarios, I find that the best thing to do is to give that person their space. Lots of space. No, more . . . more . . . more. Most freak-show train-wreck incidents are people like you and me having a bad day. They just need a chance to chill out and reflect. Give them that space and most times they'll come back to you. They'll realize the error of their ways and apologize in their own way. They'll also address the original issue. "Yeah, don't worry about the cat," they'll say, "either he's back in his body or it's Bill Johnston, our former dentist. Either way, our pet has a soul and can possibly save us hundreds on a deep clean."

A freak-show train wreck is not always to blame

Sometimes the feedback you get *is* reasonable and it resonates, but it's not easy to hear. This is the time to remember that you are not your material. You are not your approach. You are not your manners. And you are not your opinions or ideas. You are the divine creation of life manifested as you on this planet. You weave in and out of material and

Comediology

content like a fish through deep and shallow waters—always changing. Therefore, when someone gives you feedback, they are giving you an opportunity to improve on the *content* or *approach* of what you provided, not *you*. Content can be changed. The approach can be improved. And if you're open and non-defensive, you can understand, realize, and improve through this feedback. Take it as a gift because that's exactly what it is.

When you get defensive, you shut down the opportunity to improve yourself. Even if it's coming from a freak-show train wreck and it has nothing to do with you, by getting defensive, you're missing out on free entertainment. Don't do this. Business can be tough; don't make it even more difficult on yourself. Be open and willing to learn, or laugh, and you will realize, more and more, that feedback is not hurtful but is a powerful tool to help you improve your game. In fact, there is a strong likelihood that the person giving you the feedback wants you to succeed and believes in your ability to change. Otherwise, why would they invest their time in you?

Summary

Remember, when witnessing a freak-show train wreck, if you can just pretend that life is one big movie and you're getting this entertainment for free, as opposed to getting your biscuits in a tizzy, you'll be way ahead of the game. Take a step back and realize, it's not about you.

Also, when it comes to receiving feedback . . .

1) **Separate you from your material.** You are only driving this bus, you don't own it. Do your best not to hit chipmunks and the occasional armadillo, sure, but remember, you and your material are separate entities.

2) **Listen to the feedback**. Find constructive and helpful ways to improve your material, but stop there. Don't hop aboard the train to Crazy Town by taking it personally and reacting. Just observe, improve, rinse, and repeat.

3) **Take feedback as a gift**. Imagine you're a plant with roots under the surface. If you hit a rock and then recoil into anger, you've stunted any chance for extension. However, if you take this as a positive, you can use this indicator to adjust accordingly and you'll continue to progress. As it pertains to feedback, take it as a gift. As it pertains to anger, "let it go to grow."

The sign said "eight items or less." So I changed my name to Less.

—Steven Wright

Less Is More

Okay, so there was this guy and he was talking to his wife. No, wait, wait. She was talking to him and he couldn't hear her. Yeah, yeah, I think that's right. No wait, *he* was talking to *her*. No, I told it wrong. Well, I guess it doesn't matter. Anyway, he can't hear her and so she gets mad and he was like, "Uhhh . . . okay, what do you want me to do?" So then the wife said. . . wait, no, I told it wrong.

The joke that wasn't. We've all been there. We may have been the "joke" teller, as optimistic as that sounds. Or, we were the unfortunate audience. But, like walking into your parent's bedroom when you hear "scary animal sounds," either role is equally unpleasant.

The "joke" is obviously very top of mind and not well thought out. As a result, the joke teller stumbles around like Donald Trump desperately trying to recall the words to the National Anthem, leaving the audience member awkwardly frozen, like me *after* I found out how "scary animal sounds" are made.

Once the punch line, or whatever that thing was, is delivered, the audience member quickly pounces on it with forced laughter to stomp out the awkwardness. "MMMhhhaaaaa! Oh my gosh! LOL! Yes, that is *too* funny!!! Oh yes, it was the police officer—mmmmhhhhaaaa yeahhh!!!"

When anyone says "LOL" out loud to you after you've told a "joke," two things are certain. First, the joke was not a hit. Second, this person is weird.

We've all been victims of this at one time or another. With a little forethought and preparation, however, the joke could have been so easily communicated, understood, and enjoyed:

"My wife says I need to see the doctor 'cause I'm losing my hearing. But I think that's just nature's way of telling me that I don't need to listen to her anymore."

Chris S. Tabish with Kurtis Matthews

Less is more. I know, it's so contrary to the wise adage we grew up on—"super-size it." But it's true. And nowhere is this concept more obvious than in comedy.

As a comedian, you must continually refine and distill your material until you have the raw essence of the joke in as few words as possible. The numbers support this. A professional comedian will target four to six laughs per minute. If they are spending all their time with a premise, they'll have precious little time to hit their punch quota. But even at a conceptual level, they are creating a world for other people, and the more "umm"s, "ahhh"s, and awkward pauses they put in, the higher the likelihood that they will cause confusion, frustration, or worst of all, a pity giggle.

A joke, just like the plot of a gripping movie, has buildup and suspense. You set the premise and you introduce characters and facts necessary to move the plot along. Any extraneous details provided in the set up will cause drag and reduce the impact. You must tell the audience where to focus. Does the character have gnome-like feet with furry knuckles? And, more important, does it matter? If details are provided, they must be relevant to the punch line. The best comedy is simple. It's pure. It's stripped down to the core of what is required for the setup and punch.

Think about your first crush.

Your fantasy was specific and included only those key details that were crucial to the plot. For starters, you imagined them, alone. They were lying down in a candlelit room, waiting for you on a velvety plush couch. Their eyes were ablaze; they were aching with desire for your touch. You approached them slowly, ever so slowly, while the melodic sounds of Barry White seductively echoed in the background. For those of you not familiar, Barry White was the proverbial "Spanish fly" of soul. Spanish fly was a concoction that would make the object of your desire desperately yearn for you. Then, unfortunately, Google came out, revealing that Spanish fly was just really expensive sugar water and Barry White had diabetes.

Now I'd better pause before I need to publish this book under a different genre. I'm not sure what that would be exactly—"Erotic Comedy" or "Comedic Erotica"? Hmmm . . . Zach Galifianakis in bodystocking lingerie? Anyone?

The point is, the details of your fantasy were pertinent to the desire, outcome, or objective. Yes, people will tell you that they want to know

Comediology

everything. But you, as the source of comedy, have a goal—to make them laugh as much as you possibly can. You simply cannot do this with all the detail. It will bore and annoy your audience and dilute your objective. Distilling, editing, and refining is the path. Less is more.

Comediology

Like comedy, business requires a focus on specific initiatives and goals. How successful is the business that focuses on everything at the same time? I couldn't tell you. I've never heard of them.

Whether at the macro level of running the business or the micro level of running a meeting, the ability to make an impact is tied to the ability to direct your and the team's efforts. You must get down to specifics and be able to focus item by item, point by point. Where do you want your employees, bosses, and peer's attention? Do you want them just to be aware of the details, or do you want them to take action? Do they need to do it at 4 p.m. today or is "whenever they get to it" fine? Do they want tuna fish sandwiches or PB&Js with the crusts cut off?

We've all been in useless meetings reminiscent of the never-ending joke. The presenter is speaking to a PowerPoint Presentation. Or is it a Jackson Pollock painting with words? He's talking about, well, something. He has no inflection in his voice. And the words he uses have no correlation to the diarrhea blast of acronyms being presented. Sometimes, as a bonus, he reads the paragraph on the slide aloud, verbatim. Awwwwkwaaarrrddd.

On and on and on it goes. If only one knew where to focus? On him, or the entire lava vomit of Webster's dictionary being presented? What am I doing in this meeting? What's the point?!

Your mind asks these questions as you rapidly lose interest and motivation. Of course, these types of meetings are par for the course, so you must maintain the façade. You strategically squint your eyes and nod appraisingly, as if to say, "Oh yeah, the infrastructure compliant scalability PMT, I know exactly what he's talking about. . . ."

"Wait, what the *&()& is he talking about?!" Your frustration continues to mount, as does your boredom. You drift off to endeavor in more strategic inquiries. "Hmmm . . . I wonder if Herb from accounting has ever worn a rainbow-colored tutu *outside* of work?"

Chris S. Tabish with Kurtis Matthews

The seemingly endless presentation finally forwards to the only slide that actually makes sense. It's the last one that, mercifully, has only two words: "Thank You." There is the blaring sound of silence as people realize that, at last, the gangrenous molar has been extracted. Thanks again Bill Johnston, Dentist-Cat!

I hope you've never been in a meeting like this but, alas, I'm sure you have. It happens all the time. Countless, precious hours of our existence are continually wasted year after year on these pointless events.

Conversely, each one of us has also witnessed, and even led, a very effective meeting. One example where *everyone* has done this is when we're returning merchandise. Let's go point by point on this exciting journey together, shall we? I know, it's returning merchandise at a store! But, trust me, it's an example of one of the most effective meetings we've ever had. Oh yeah, and for this example, you can *totally* bypass standing in line behind Grandma Ferguson, who is evidently returning every Christmas gift since 1954. Ahhh . . . don't you just love imaginary merchandise returns? Here's what it looks like:

Clerk: Hi, welcome to WalrusMart. Sadly, we're all out of clams, but how may I help you?

You: Cut the crap, you! Put those nasty E.T. fingers in that drawer and give me back my cash for these chocolate-coated fecal treats you sold me. What in the hell were you people thinking?! While you're at it, wipe that Norman Bates corporate smile off your face, you creepy Stephen King character, you!

Okay, okay, so maybe that's me fantasizing again. In real life, it's probably more like this:

You: Hi, I'd made a purchase here and I'd like to return it.

While I find the first example so much more fun to imagine, the important thing to realize is that, either way, you're off to an effective meeting.

First, you have an objective.

The key here is that you've put thought into the objective *before* the meeting. Because of this, you know exactly *who* you need to have with you in the meeting—the return clerk. And, if the clerk has his head up a squatting kangaroo's backside, the store manager. You don't invite the person who sold you the merchandise or the person who was in line after you. And you don't include Judy, pronounced, "Judilia," your victimized

Comediology

neighbor, who just knows the "man" is dragging you down. Clearly these people are unnecessary to your objective and they will only create confusion, weirdness or worse, a staph infection.

Think of the times when you've been invited to a meeting for no apparent reason. It's frustrating and it wastes people's time. The problem comes in when there is no clear objective. In that case, we tend to invite more people because we erroneously think all of them can somehow help us see the light in a sea of ambiguity. They can't. In fact, they'll just make things worse by offering more opinions you don't need, further confusing the topic. *Less is more.*

But to get there, you must plan for it up front. Moreover, you must resist the temptation of "more." What if this merchandise return gets me to a higher tax bracket? Perhaps my accountant and a representative from the IRS should be there. As you can see, this is how corporate-meeting misery begins. Don't take a bite of that apple. Resist the temptation.

Second, you've stated the objective.

"I'd like to make a return." Congratulations, you're now better off than 99.97 percent of the meetings out there. You've articulated what you want and you've done this up front in a very clear and concise manner. Everyone now knows what success looks like. It's simple. If you get the return, as Borat would say, "Meeting is great success, very excite!" If you don't, well, it's not. You didn't dance around with a "Errrr, well, what do *you* guys think should be on the agenda?" No, because that isn't a meeting. It's a blog, or a YouTube video, or, better yet, a passing thought that you never tell ANYONE. EVER.

Third, you effectively used visuals.

Nancy Duarte is a TED speaker and founder of Duarte, an amazing presentation design, strategy, and training company. For reference, Duarte closely worked with Al Gore on the documentary *An Inconvenient Truth*. For those that have seen the film, you understand the use of slide show visuals, their amazing power when done effectively and also that grandma's hairspray killed three types of porpoises, a few lemurs, and the entire ozone layer.

Nancy has coined a term: "the Glance Test." This states that an audience should be able to understand the point of your visual presentation in three

Chris S. Tabish with Kurtis Matthews

seconds or less. This has two implications. First, it requires the audience to be focused on your visual. In other words, you're not splitting their attention. Imagine an example where a slide depicts one topic, but the presenter is talking about a completely separate topic altogether. . The auditory portion of the audience is listening to the presenter's words thinking of one thing. The visual portion of the audience is looking at the presentation and thinking of something completely different. And the portion that's already checked out is trying to figure out how to retrieve their dentist-cat's soul from the vacuum bag. To avoid splitting the audience's focus and therefore confusing them, present one focus at one time. Now, let's get back to the returns counter:

> **Clerk:** May I see the item?
> **You:** Yes, here's the item.
> [the clerk inspects the item]
> **You**: And here's the accompanying receipt.
> [the clerk reviews the receipt]

The second implication is that your visuals are easy to grasp quickly. In the above example, the returned item provided the visual, illustrating the specific focus. You didn't talk while the clerk was inspecting the item. Right? RIGHT?! No, you let the clerk *focus* on the visual you provided.

Once the clerk had inspected the item, you then went to your next visual, the receipt. Again, you didn't talk while the clerk was inspecting the receipt, instead allowing time for the clerk to *focus* on your visual.

This is just one of many great examples of a very effective meeting you may have led. You knew your audience and included pertinent members only. You presented the salient points. You focused the audience on one thing at a time. And you provided them memorable visuals that supported the presentation. Other examples include meeting with a doctor when you're sick, going to the bank to withdraw money, and calling 911 because your cat's soul has now escaped from the vacuum bag, climbed an invisible tree, and is now performing root canals on squirrels.

Comediology

Summary

Set yourself up for productive meetings. Make them simple and effective. Remember that you've led countless numbers of effective meetings in everyday life. Use these experiences to make your meetings in business successful as well.

1) **Have a clear objective.** State the known objective up front so that everyone in the meeting knows what success looks like. This will help attendees contribute in a productive way, which will move you toward your goal and also make them feel like they're adding value. Oh what a feeling, they're dancing on the ceiling.

2) **Only add those people directly pertinent to the meeting.** In other words, have mercy.

3) **Use effective visuals.** Be sure to connect visuals with your words for the greatest impact. Remember Nancy Duarte's "Glance Test." Your audience should be able to understand the point of your visual presentation in three seconds or less.

4) **Focus on one point at a time.** Don't distract your audience with too many points. As we all know, this was the main catalyst that caused apes to rule our planet in an alternate reality. See what I mean?

You're only given a little spark of madness. You mustn't lose it.

—Robin Williams

Finding Your Voice

When I started in comedy, I wanted to be just like the comedians I idolized. I wanted to portray characters just like Robin Williams, be observationally brilliant like Jerry Seinfeld, and also pack Sam Kinison's jolt. I worked hard at emulating their acts. In fact, there was only one major difference between theirs and mine: theirs were funny.

Okay, maybe that's a bit harsh. There was that one time. Or maybe I was just really gassy? Regardless, even in the best moment, it was just that. A moment. It was nice to make people laugh, but it felt like it was only possible with a mask. I felt like I was wearing an identity that was not my own. I felt like if they saw the real person I was, they would see I'm not really like that. And, in all candor, I wasn't. I was only doing it as an act to get them to laugh because I love bringing joy to people. I just didn't want to "expose" myself to do it.

You see, I didn't want people to know about, well, me. It was quite a strange phenomenon, but I suppose not all that uncommon. I wanted to be funny. I wanted to entertain. And I really wanted to connect through this mechanism of comedy. That said, I was desperately fearful of people finding out "the truth."

And just what was "the truth"? Good question; I can't say I was sure. At the time, I was having an identity crisis. On one hand, I had a "proper" identity. Let's call it the Clark Kent or "nerd" persona. In this role, I was "supposed" to be a Silicon Valley Professional—serious, left-brained and, well, let's be honest, kind of a douche canoe. I was really good at that last part, by the way. I was fearful that if people knew that I did stand-up comedy, somehow my persona, and perhaps my career, would be at risk:

"Hey, did you hear that Chris is doing comedy? How could we possibly trust him with improving our operational throughput?! Isn't this thing, this 'comedy' what caused the *Titanic* to sink, the *Hindenburg* to explode,

Chris S. Tabish with Kurtis Matthews

and ultimately was the culprit for our laptop cameras to turn on and spontaneously FaceTime live all our friends during quality "alone" time?

On the other hand, I was a "comedian." Well, kind of. I was on stage posing as a comedian, but I was definitely different from the other comedians. For example, I was one of the few performers who was actually employed. Put simply, I had sold out to the man! I was a professional business person, aka corporate tightwad—douche canoe. Who was *I*, of all people, to be funny on stage?! I had an MBA and referred to myself as an "executive." I actually used words like "process re-engineering" and "robust" *in sentences*! And not just to make fun of other corporate douche canoes. Last I checked, these are not the credentials that get you onto HBO's Comedy Hour.

It was obvious that I was different, even in the way I looked. I resembled the guy that comedians made fun of, not one of the performers. In fact, as an opener, I would often jokingly apologize to the crowd, "Sorry for sporting the 'employed look' this evening. I hope it doesn't come between us."

A True Comedian, whatever the hell that means, was, at least in my mind, a borderline addict who didn't love his parents and burned every local educational institution to the ground by the age of seven. He was raised by abusive, misguided souls named Starchild and Body Glisten. He ultimately escaped the nudist camp by grinding his teeth to a sharp edge, enabling him to chew through the ropes. He then stole a car, and started a brief, but evidently very effective, drinking habit, which led him to Al's Night Club, where he was discovered by Lorne Michaels. This was clearly not my path.

Suffice to say, not only did I aspire to be like the comedian greats of old, but I *needed* to be them, because, let's be honest, I couldn't be myself. And now, this was impacting both worlds, I couldn't be myself in the stand-up world because I was a professional. Likewise, I couldn't be myself in my professional world because I was a comedian. I was "swimming with my boots on" in all aspects of life.

So, the effect was this. When I was funny, it was only fleeting. I could emulate the greats momentarily, but I couldn't *be* them. Consequently, I didn't want to invite people to my shows. First off, I would have to get past

Comediology

the shell shock of telling them that I did stand-up. Second, they would see that it really wasn't me up there. Weird.

Despite my identity crisis, I did have a moment of bravery. This courageousness came at a time when my "act" was performing a specific character. I know, someone other than me . . . shocking. I had been developing the character for some time and he offered two positive aspects. First, he had people laughing, in class at least, and second, he enabled me to hide two feet behind him.

As a result of this "in-class success," I was encouraged by Kurtis to enter the "The Battle of the Bay" Stand-Up Comedy Competition. Perhaps someday I'll forgive him. After much deliberation and three Coronas later, I decided to enter. Well, it was my name on the form anyway. God only knew who exactly would be on stage. He, however, was unavailable for comment.

Once I signed up, I learned the rules. The winner of the competition would be determined by how much the audience liked their performance, judged by how loud they cheered for it. Therefore, as a comedian, the more people you invited, the better chance you had of winning. What?! Why couldn't we just do what I've always done and passed a note—"Do you think I'm cute or funny? Please check a box."

This was a dauntingly huge step for me. To date, I had only begun to let people know that I performed comedy as a hobby, much less actually invited them to a show. And now, I had to make my way out of the closet. Why should gay people be the only ones with a place to hide? I reluctantly invited several people I knew socially and even asked a couple of people from work. "Wanna come to a comedy show?" I would ask, followed quickly by "I'll be performing and, you know, there'll probably be some funny people there, too."

In retrospect, I'm embarrassed to realize how self-centered this perspective was. After all, we're all walking around thinking about ourselves, not one another. Why would anyone ever spend any time thinking of me and my comedian/professional conflict when clearly there are so many intriguing dog food labels to read? Ash? What?! You people are putting ash into dog food?! Seriously? Oh, and here's another question, dog food industry—thousands of types of foods and toys, but not one of them is poop flavored? This is a serious gap in the market, people!

Chris S. Tabish with Kurtis Matthews

Back to the story at hand. If the situation had ever been mathematically calculated, no doubt it would be revealed that my associates spent more time thinking about the phenomena of vacuuming cat souls than me and my identity dilemma. But hey, that's what happens when we let "Rocko," the crazed, and often naked, egomaniac, residing in the Frontal Lobe Apartments, take the wheel.

The big night finally came. The turnout was huge. There were hundreds of people in the audience. I was so nervous. It felt like my lower intestine was a jump rope at a Big and Tall Convention. I wanted to make the audience sign a disclaimer before I went on stage. Something like, "Chris has no idea what the hell he's doing. Like former president Clinton, he just wanted to put his lips around some comedy but not really 'inhale.' Thus, in no way should this incident remain associated with his identity because, after all, 'it isn't really him.' In other words, 'it was Beence!'"

But, alas, there was no lawyer in sight and I had apparently forgotten how to form words and sentences. My name was called to the stage. Actually, scratch that. I didn't even use my real name. I used one of my character names and *he* was called to the stage. Now, this particular character is a highly-engineered concoction of mostly dumb, sprinkled together with some dimwittedness. He has an overwhelming sex drive and is even charming. You know, if senseless half-wits with bad teeth are your thing. His name is Horry Moates and he is literally cross-eyed, looking like he's stuck between two states—inebriated and Arkansas.

With Horry, it often takes a moment for the "funny" to come. When it does, it's when the audience realizes that he's just a character and there's no way someone could actually be "that stupid." Typically this recognition occurs as he describes his finer qualities, "I'm a quarter Jeep Cherokee," he spouts, "so I'm pretty powerful going up hills."

At this point, they see that they no longer need to hold the obligatory forced smile and large-eyed, sympathetic gaze. "Oh, I got it," they think, "he's a jackass on purpose. We can shamelessly point and laugh at him." Meanwhile, Horry, unaware of the intelligence assessment in progress, continues with a smooth, pick-up line: "Maybe you and I could get something to eat after the show. You like oysters? I hear they're a natural herm-aphrodisiac. Oh yeah."

Comediology

Once they realize that this is a caricature, they start laughing. This, in turn, gives other audience members permission as well.

This is the typical set for Horry Moates. For reasons unknown to me, however, this day was different. No one, and I mean NO ONE laughed. Perhaps people thought that Horry was "special" and were fearful of hurting his feelings. Or maybe this true and tried material just wasn't funny for this audience. Hundreds of people sat in silent judgment as Horry spewed his material to a stone wall. It was completely awkward and embarrassing. And oddly as it sounds, it even felt downright shameful.

The real problem was, I couldn't stop the act. Up to that point, all I had *ever* performed on stage was characters or emulations of other comedians. This time, however, that wouldn't work. As odd as it sounds, I didn't know how to be "just me" on stage. Therefore, I had to keep going. I couldn't just stop, take off the proverbial mask, and be like, "Well, that was awkward, now let's start some real comedy." I simply didn't know how.

What was I going to talk about while I was just "being me"? To be a comedian, you need a point of view, an opinion. At the office, I had always followed the politically correct convention—aka "the herd" or, more specifically, the tightwad in front of me—and therefore never gave myself permission to have an opinion, especially out loud and in public. This definitely posed a conflict on stage. Sure, I wanted to be funny and make people laugh, but I didn't have this key prerequisite—or, more properly, I hadn't yet unleashed it. Consequently, I had to rely on a synthetic or watered-down version of myself portraying a character or emulating someone else. For all intents and purposes, as it pertained to me, *the real me*, I was a newborn.

So, as painful as it was, I continued on that night as Horry. And let me tell you, this was *the* longest prostate exam. *Ever.* My only other option was to stare stupidly out in space until my time was up. Which, in retrospect, may have been a better choice.

I got off stage. I went home. I rolled around in some self-loathing, followed by shame, followed by some Ben and Jerry's. I consoled myself by saying "it wasn't really all that bad." Then I called a couple of friends, who tried to console me by saying, "It wasn't really all that bad." Which, of course led me to the undisputed conclusion that it *was* "really all that bad."

I can't lie. Realizing that my act didn't work in front of hundreds of people was a very painful experience. I seriously considered quitting. Why should I do something that gives me anxiety and self-doubt? It was a very insecure time for me. I wanted to be funny on stage, but I was slowly realizing that this would require me to reveal my identity. I wanted to be me. I wanted to be original and authentic but I didn't know how. I wanted to have an act that was formed on opinions and observations that were my own. I witnessed other comedian's profound moments. I could see their genuine selves. I envied that. But how was I going to do this? I needed to change.

Actually, scratch that. I didn't need to change but rather, I needed to give myself a chance to be me, just the way I was. So what if it didn't meet the politically correct standard? So what if it wasn't funny? In a very weird and circuitous route, this experience made me realize that, regardless of the outcome, it was most important to be real, to be genuine, to be me.

Since that time, I have opened the floodgates, let myself out on stage, and given myself permission to roam free. Some days it flows naturally, and other days it requires a bran muffin. But it's always authentic, always genuine, always me. Yes, there are days when I bomb on stage—HUGE "cow fart" catastrophes. On these days, while I know I didn't hit it out of the park, I still walk away with the self-respect of knowing I put myself out there, which to me, means a lot. Then, there are those days where I *do* hit it out of the park. My material comes alive and I connect with the audience in a flurry of laughter. It's amazing. I feel the genuine connection with them because *I'm* genuine. It feels like we're co-creating this world of complete joy together. This authentic connection and co-creation would not have been possible if I had not been the genuine article, because the only way you can connect with other people is when you reveal your true self.

Ultimately, for me, this did not require a massive search. More than anything else, it meant turning off, or at least down, my internal critic. Once I did that, my true self was revealed by default.

Everyone has a unique gift of engagement, a way to communicate with another human being that is specific to them. It's their authentic inner voice. Since this gift is different for each individual, it makes no sense to compare yours to others and criticize yourself where you don't think you "measure up." On the contrary, you must believe in it. You must invest in it. And you must encourage it. Most importantly, however, to find it and watch it grow, you must set it free.

I won't lie. It's scary. Sometimes you're going to say and do things the kid inside you who still believes in heaven just wouldn't approve of. And that's okay. No, really. You're not going to cease to exist. You will go on. I promise. More important, you'll experience and explore what it's like to be the real you. You're going to learn of new preferences, new strengths, and even new gifts you never knew you had.

Comediology

In my career, while I had leadership capabilities, I was quite adept at being a "first follower." At work I would readily grasp both the written and tribal rules, assimilate them, and then walk the line. I was effective in my job, but only to a point. You really can't push beyond existing boundaries to make significant progress if you're only willing to go as far as the people next to you. Comedy helped me realize that I had not given myself permission to hold my own opinions, preferences, and practices. I had not ventured out, or shall I say "in," to explore the real me.

The "first follower" approach got me things—raises, promotions, and several employee awards. Once highly coveted, they're now best described as "dusty." And while I appreciated them, they never really fulfilled me. How could they? I was basically being rewarded for "adapting." And while I was good at emulating corporate leaders, this approach severely limited me to their way of thinking, interacting, and being. Worst of all, by doing this, I was always externally focused. I wasn't looking inward to *my* voice for guidance.

In spite of this, my voice did call out at times, or more accurately, just wouldn't shut up. "I'm here, let me out. Being an android is not doing it for me! We should be doing something else!" If my mind was the government, my inner voice was Martin Luther King Jr. It constantly protested. I responded by tightly locking down both my larynx and sphincter, his only two means of escape. "You've got a good job," I would tell him. "People count on you. You make good money and you have a very competent cat-dentist most people couldn't afford. You've got this."

Chris S. Tabish with Kurtis Matthews

There are two problems with this approach. First, you never really get to live life as your genuine self, which means you never discover what *you* are all about. And second, lattes are *way* more expensive than self-esteem. We are here to *experience* life, not *adapt* to it. What *could* I do if I lived out my deepest desire? What possibilities were out there? And how could I explore them if, every time I was on the cusp of an amazing self-discovery that would achieve my soul's desire, I was interrupted by Judy from accounting, who positively required my TPS report to be submitted by noon?

Comedy helped me realize that I had not given myself permission to live authentically, as the genuine article. It helped me realize this on stage but also in my career. So many times, I had been in a meeting where I wasn't myself. Sure, people wanted me to be—pragmatic, reasonable, agreeable, and so on. But what did *I* think about it? I wasn't sure, and I was so deep into pleasing others that I hadn't even allowed myself permission to explore it.

I want to clarify a point here. I'm all for helping someone by doing their bidding. In my opinion, being in humble service to others is one of the most selfless and admirable things you can do in this life. That said, I strongly advocate that this service is best done as yourself. People can, and hopefully will, tell you what they want. But after that, it's your authentic self, taking it in and determining the path forward.

In my corporate role, it went something like this. My boss and their peers are in this meeting. They've come up with a proposal and, well, *I* like getting paid, so *I'm* agreeable. Now, within the bounds of "agreeable corporate guy," I could then engage my brain. "Oh, well Jane, that's a great idea, and what if we did this to further support it." "Well done, Chris, I'll be sure your payroll check has no extra deductions this week."

Like being "stuck" on stage emulating something that wasn't me, I would also get stuck in this corporate role. If a meeting became anything *but* agreeable, I found it very difficult to switch contexts. How could I push back on my boss and her peers while I was "agreeable corporate guy"? Likewise, if an effort required "out of the box" thinking, forget it. How can you possibly suggest a strong action that might offend the people you're supposed to be agreeing with? It was like playing the lead in a James Bond movie. At a crucial action scene where I needed to do a double-somersault

136

Comediology

spin-kick flip, I would look down and realize I wasn't James Bond after all but, in fact, Winnie the Pooh. Instead of pulling out a can of whoop-ass, I would instead reach for my jar of honey while saying to myself, "think, think, think . . . they're all full of pooh but I'll say nothing and remain employed. Yes! That's the thing to do."

The problem wasn't the dynamic, challenging environment. In fact, this is the one of the things I truly did enjoy. The problem was me trying to "play a role" instead of being present with my own voice.

I knew the possibility existed. I've witnessed people who were in touch with their authenticity, their true voice. I've deeply envied them. They say what they mean and they mean what they say. And you can tell that they're not just "toeing the line" or "playing a role." This is genuinely who they are.

My friend Martin Shervington calls this being "bulletproof." This means that if you don't give a hoot what people think but hold yourself in the highest regard, the proverbial bullets can't hurt you. He's right. The way I look at it is this. It's either perfect. Or it's not. Either way, it's perfect.

But, wait a minute, how can something be "perfect" when it's "not perfect"? It's like this. It's perfect because we've acknowledged that it's *not* perfect. And the only way we know it's not perfect is because we know ourselves. We've bounced it up against our true selves, not an emulation or an act, mind you. And we've asked the question, "Hey, is this perfect?"

If it resonates with us, if we can feel it in our bones, then yes, it's perfect and it doesn't matter what anyone else says because that's it. It's real. It's done and you *know.*

Conversely, if it's not perfect, you know at that moment. It's like the time I tried to do a handstand to impress my future wife. But instead of gracefully positioning my weight on my arms, I fell flat on my back, which knocked the wind out of me and left me desperately, and embarrassingly, gasping for air in front of a crowd of about twenty-five people. In that moment, I could honestly say that impressing her with my physical prowess was probably not the perfect road to drive Miss Daisy.

It's like having an internal critic that's always on. He identifies and informs you of anything that doesn't resonate with your true self early. Once identified, you make the choice that's right for you. You can do this in any situation without being arrogant, dismissive, or rude. It just doesn't resonate with you, that's all. You can either "correct" it or walk away. The point is, you're free of this imperfect thing. You don't need to continue playing a part that doesn't fit you. And you know *now*, not two bad career choices from now. And *that's* why it's perfect.

The problem comes in when we don't know something is imperfect because we aren't present enough to find our true voice in the situation. Or when we simply ignore the signs and let our minds justify moving forward: "Sure, I hate this job with every fiber in my body. But soon, I'll get a 10 percent raise and buy a Dodge Stratus. *Then,* I'll be truly happy."

If you've found your true voice and are present, you'll realize that this situation and others like it are not right for you and you need to run the for the door. If they don't bring you joy and fulfillment and don't resonate with who you are, why continue with them?

At one point when I was deep in the large intestine of "working for the man," I recall thinking, "Yes, I'm miserable at my job, but I'm making enough money to save for my kid's college fund. So even if I live a miserable existence, they can go to college and live their dreams."

"Wait a minute," says your internal critic. "What the @#!@ are you thinking?! If you're not living your dreams, what makes you think they're going to do so? The example you're setting, and the one that they're seeing, is their father repressing himself. With an example like that, what makes you think they're going to live life differently?" And you know what, he was right.

I realized that if I want my children to take their shot and live their dreams, while being true to their selves, I'd better start doing so. Even if that means I don't "make it," I've found my inner voice and am living life in accordance to it. I'm living by my rules and not by someone else's. And by doing this and this alone, regardless of the outcome, I have "made it." It's like Thomas Jefferson said, "I prefer dangerous freedom over peaceful slavery." (I can only hope he didn't write that while in bed with a slave).

That said, I truly believe if we listen to our inner voice, it will lead us to great places. We were meant for awe-inspiring greatness. Living small and doing things to solely to please others, while sacrificing ourselves, does not serve us or anyone around us. It is important to note that there is a difference between "pleasing" and "serving." When you *please* others, you aim to gain their acceptance. However, when you *serve* others, you aim to share your fulfillment and joy with them. Find and listen to your

Comediology

inner voice, your light. Then, share it and let it shine on and enlighten others. I think Marianne Williamson puts it best in a piece often titled "Our Greatest Fear":

It is our light not our darkness that most frightens us.
Our deepest fear is not that we are inadequate.
Our deepest fear is that we are powerful beyond measure.
It is our light not our darkness that most frightens us.
We ask ourselves, who am I to be brilliant, gorgeous,
talented and fabulous?

Actually, who are you not to be?
You are a child of God.
Your playing small does not serve the world.
There's nothing enlightened about shrinking so that other
people won't feel insecure around you.

We were born to make manifest the glory of
God that is within us.

It's not just in some of us; it's in everyone.
And as we let our own light shine,
we unconsciously give other people
permission to do the same.

As we are liberated from our own fear,
Our presence automatically liberates others.

Summary

You really can't push beyond existing boundaries to make significant progress if you're only willing to go as far as the people next to you. To advance, you need not search externally but internally. Look inside to find your core, your authentic self, and from there, simply listen and nurture.

1) **Actively evaluate your life to see if circumstances resonate with you.** If they don't, change them now rather than several jobs and decades later.

2) **Be an inspiration for yourself and generations to come.** Do this by living in accordance with your authentic self. Reinforce to yourself and let others know that, not only is it "OK" but, in fact, is the only way to truly live.

3) **Live to "serve," not to "please."** When you please others, you aim to gain their acceptance. However, when you serve others, you aim to share your fulfillment and joy with them.

4) **Living small does not serve you.** In fact, it serves no one. Let your true self shine and show others the way. Do not fear this transition. It is only as scary as you make it out to be. Embrace this transition and watch miracles occur.

In the end, everything is a gag.

—Charlie Chaplin

Epilogue

Life takes us on journeys that we never anticipated or, quite frankly, ever wanted. For me, the key has been keeping myself open to joy while being on a different path than the one I expected. There is joy and fulfillment in every path; I just have to be open to receiving it. Comedy has helped me realize this.

As it turns out, stand-up comedy has been a great catalyst for me, but not a destination, at least not professionally. Don't get me wrong, I still love getting up on stage and it brings me joy to make people laugh, but this is not my career path.

Over the course of my journey, I came to realize that I really do love helping people in corporations with their biggest challenges. This typically involves some type of technological transformation. And while technology is the headline, the real transformation lies with people.

To that end, comedy remains a valuable tool for me in helping people open up to new ideas and possibilities. It also has been key in bringing people closer together through shared laughter and acknowledgment of our common ideals and struggles.

Most importantly, I feel that comedy has helped me find, well, me. It has helped me see the truth, laugh about and even find joy in it, and then move on, thereby not getting stuck in a state of denial.

I hope this book has helped you do the same—open up, laugh, find joy and fulfillment, and, along the way, maybe even yourself. Because being true to your own self, your own voice, is the only true and right path for *you*.

So, that's a wrap. In summary—what's that? You didn't like it? Which parts? Please tell me! I'll totally rewrite it for you. No, seriously, tell me what you need me to be. I'll change everything. Just *like* me. PLEASE!

Acknowledgments

Whether or not they'll actually admit to it after reading this book, the following people had a significant influence, helped create it or inspired me along the way and I want to thank them from the bottom of my soul. Wait a minute, doesn't the bottom have all that residue and stuff? Okay, well, scratch that. I want to thank them from the top of my soul. . .

Leta Tabish; amazing, wonderful, and beautiful children Jackson, Lucy, and Charlie Tabish; Joyce Firestack; Denny and Marty Brown; Matt and Mikey Brown; Kirk and Ashley Brown; Brent Brown; Rosemary Brown; Rich and Kathy Brown; Bret Croft; David Nihill; Martin Shervington; Greg and Margie Abbott; Steve and Tiffany Stock; Ellen Terwilliger; Michelle Bhatia; JuneAn Lanigan; Rebecca Burnside; Jamie Johnson; the Ten Bosch family; Saura Naim; Sunny and Ranjna Bedi; Piper Cole; Aaron and Tina Wilkins; Raghu Kidambi; Travis and Jenny Snyder; Bill Mandarino; Tyler and Emily Jones; Mark and Lynne Muir; Jason and Paige Berg; Jeff Popp; the Zeal family; Jason Incorvaia; Michele Goins; Jason Hsieh; Huib and Maria Ponssen; Erin Mahoney; the Kumar family; Jay Pillai; James Fraleigh (wonderful job eddettingg); Priscilla Rice and James Ward (audiobook recording and editing); Bruce Fabric; Rebecca Burnside; John and Rebecca Wallemen; Linda Subryan; Robert and Cheryl Roffey; Bob Sadler; Bruce Regenhardt, Mark Schwartz and Wally Grivois.

Sources

American Physiological Society. "Anticipating a Laugh Reduces Our Stress Hormones, Study Shows." *ScienceDaily*, April 10, 2008. www. sciencedaily.com/releases/2008/04/080407114617.htm.

Biddle, Sam. "The 10 Greatest (Accidental) Inventions of All Time." *NBC News,* 2012, accessed July 2, 2018. http://www.nbcnews.com/ id/38870091/ns/technology_and_science-innovation/t/greatest-accidental-inventions-all-time/#.WHurtLGZNE4.

Casciaro, Tiziana, and Miguel Sousa Lobo. "Competent Jerks, Lovable Fools, and the Formation of Social Networks. *Harvard Business Review,* June 2005. https://hbr.org/2005/06/ competent-jerks-lovable-fools-and-the-formation-of-social-networks.

Cyran, Pamela, and Chris Gaylord. "The 20 Most Fascinating Accidental Inventions." *Christian Science Monitor,* October 5, 2012. http://www. csmonitor.com/Technology/2012/1005/The-20-most-fascinating-accidental-inventions/Chocolate-chip-cookies.

Dr. Seuss. *The Sneetches and Other Stories*. New York: Random House, 1961.

Duarte, Nancy. "Do Your Slides Pass the Glance Test?" *Harvard Business Review*, October 22, 2012. https://hbr.org/2012/10/ do-your-slides-pass-the-glance-test/.

Dunbar, R. I. M., Rebecca Baron, Anna Frangou, Eiluned Pearce, Edwin J. C. van Leeuwin, Julie Stow, Giselle Partridge, Ian MacDonald, Vincent Barra, and Mark van Vugt. "Social Laughter Is Correlated with an Elevated Pain Threshold." *Proceedings of the Royal Society B,*

September 14, 2011. http://rspb.royalsocietypublishing.org/content/early/2011/09/12/rspb.2011.1373.full.

Grant, Adam. *Originals: How Non-conformists Move the World.* New York: Penguin, 2016.

Hampson, Rick. "What You Didn't Know about King's 'Dream' Speech." *USA Today,* August 12, 2013. http://www.usatoday.com/story/news/nation/2013/08/12/march-on-washington-king-speech/2641841/.

Hoption, Colette, Julian Barling, and Nick Turner. "'It's Not You, It's Me': Transformational Leadership and Self-deprecating Humor." *Leadership & Organization Development Journal* 34, no. 1 (2013): 4–19.

Isen, A., K. Daubman, and G. Nowicki, G. "Positive Affect Facilitates Creative Problem Solving." *Journal of Personality and Social Psychology* 52, no. 6 (1987): 1122–31.

Knight, Phil. *Shoe Dog.* New York: Simon & Schuster, 2016.

"Maya Angelou on Courage and Creativity." *Harvard Business Review,* May 2013. https://hbr.org/2013/05/maya-angelou-on-courage-and-cr; background on Wikipedia: https://en.wikipedia.org/wiki/Maya_Angelou.

Medical News Today. "Laugh a Little to Help Protect Heart, Lower Blood Pressure." American College of Sports Medicine, press release. http://www.medicalnewstoday.com/releases/151941.php.

Nemo, John. "What a NASA Janitor Can Teach Us about Living a Bigger Life." *The Business Journals,* December 23, 2014. http://www.bizjournals.com/bizjournals/how-to/growth-strategies/2014/12/what-a-nasa-janitor-can-teach-us.html.

Provine, Robert. "The Science of Laughter." *Psychology Today,* November 1, 2000.

Roche, Jennifer. "What a Calligrapher Priest Taught Steve Jobs: The Art of Beautiful Writing and Technology." *National Catholic*

Register, January 19, 2012. http://www.ncregister.com/daily-news/what-a-calligrapher-priest-taught-steve-jobs.

https://www.psychologytoday.com/articles/200011/the-science-laughter.

Weems, Scott. "Does Humor Make You Smarter?" *Psychology Today,* August 15, 2014. https://www.psychologytoday.com/blog/what-s-so-funny/201408/does-humor-make-you-smarter.

Wikipedia, s.v. "I Have a Dream." Last modified June 6, 2018, 09:30. https://en.wikipedia.org/wiki/I_Have_a_Dream.

Wikipedia, s.v. "Mahalia Jackson." Last modified June 25, 2018, 01:12. https://en.wikipedia.org/wiki/Mahalia_Jackson.

About the Authors

Chris Tabish is the co-founder of Venture West Consulting in Silicon Valley whose mission is to help organizations create meaningful strategies and bring them to reality. Chris has been active in the stand-up comedy world since 2010 and continues to perform in the San Francisco Bay area where he lives with his wife Leta and three kids Jackson, Lucy and Charlie.

Kurtis Matthews is a professional comedian, executive comedy coach and stand up teacher. Kurtis starred in the hit BBC 1 Reality Show, "Find Me the Funny" as well as Season 2 of the Popular TV Show, "Celebrity Rehab with Dr. Drew". He founded the San Francisco Comedy College (SFCC), the nation's largest stand-up school.

For more information, please visit us at www.comediology.com

Made in the USA
San Bernardino, CA
27 January 2019